Living Through History

THE COLD WAR

STEPHEN ASHTON

B.T. Batsford Ltd London

CONTENTS

© Stephen Ashton 1990
First published 1990

All rights reserved. No part of this publication
may be reproduced, in any form or by any means,
without permission from the Publisher.

Typeset by Tek-Art Ltd, West Wickham, Kent
Printed and bound in Great Britain by
The Bath Press, Bath, Somerset
for the publishers
B.T. Batsford Ltd
4 Fitzhardinge Street
London W1H 0AH

ISBN 0 7134 5817 8

Acknowledgments

The Author and Publishers would like to thank the
following for their kind permission to reproduce
illustrations: Associated Press for figure 44; The
Bettman Archive for figure 1; The Camera Press
for figure 37; The Hulton Picture Library for
figures 7, 9, 13, 23, 25, 26, 32 and 35; Topham
Picture Library for figures 2, 3, 4, 5, 6, 8, 10, 11,
16, 19, 20, 22, 27, 28, 30, 31, 33, 34, 36, 38, 40, 41,
42, 43, 45. The maps included as figures 12, 15, 21,
24 and 39 were drawn by Robert Brien.

Cover Illustrations

The colour photograph shows an H-bomb test on
Bikini Atoll, 1956, (courtesy Topham Picture
Library); the bottom left photograph shows Stalin,
Truman and Churchill at the Potsdam conference,
1945 (courtesy Hulton Picture library); the bottom
right photograph shows East German police
discussing the border situation with West
Berliners through the barbed wire fencing in the
Neukoelln district, September 1961 (courtesy
Topham Picture Library).

THE COLD WAR AS HISTORY

This book examines the origins of the Cold War between the end of the Second World War in 1945 and the death of Stalin in 1953. It concentrates on Europe but it also considers how the nuclear age began when two atomic bombs were dropped on Japan. The Cold War was not confined to Europe, nor did it end in 1953. In the 50s and 60s, it was extended across the world. The final chapter of this book takes the story up to the early 60s. Specifically, it examines the background to the construction of the Berlin Wall in 1961 and the Cuban missile crisis in 1962.

The expression 'Cold War' was coined in 1947 by Walter Lippmann, an influential American journalist. Since then historians have put forward three different arguments to explain how the Cold War started. The first is the orthodox, which argues that responsibility rests with the Russians. As the first Marxist state, the Soviet Union was committed to the goal of world-wide communist expansion. Orthodox historians maintain that Hitler's invasion of the Soviet Union in 1941 forced Stalin to make a tactical alliance with the United States and Britain. The alliance was tactical because Stalin distrusted his wartime allies. He viewed the alliance purely as a means to defeat Hitler. Once the war was over, Stalin intended to use local communists in different countries as well as the Red Army to expand communism. The western powers – America more so than Britain – misread Stalin's intentions. To keep Stalin as an ally in the war, they made concessions to him in Eastern Europe. But once the war was over,

1 The 'Big Three' – Churchill, Roosevelt and Stalin – meet at Yalta in the Crimea, February 1945. Roosevelt, who relied on personal diplomacy in his dealings with Stalin, died in April 1945. Churchill was voted out of office in the summer of 1945. Stalin alone survived of the wartime allies against Hitler.

they began to see reality. As President Truman put it in 1946; 'Unless Russia is faced by an iron fist and strong language another war is in the making.' For the orthodox historians, therefore, the Cold War became a story of Western resistance against communist expansion.

The second explanation is the revisionist. Revisionist historians argue that Stalin had other priorities at the end of the war. The struggle against Hitler had taken a heavy toll. Russia lost 20 million dead and thousands of towns and villages had been destroyed. Stalin mistrusted his wartime allies but this was not surprising. The Western powers had fought against the Bolsheviks during Russia's civil war (1918-21) and they had also appeased

2 Friends and allies, but for how long? A Russian commander greets his American counterpart in Germany in May 1945.

Hitler. To defend the Soviet Union against another invasion, Stalin wanted to create a buffer zone of 'friendly' states along Russia's western frontier. For the revisionists, therefore, reconstruction and security were Stalin's main priorities.

Revisionists blame the United States for the Cold War. They argue that the Cold War developed because America wanted to impose its own domination throughout the world. America's involvement in the Vietnam War in the 1960s led the revisionists to reach this conclusion. They began by asking themselves why America was fighting in Vietnam. They traced the explanation back to the years during and after the Second World War.

The US economy expanded during the war. GNP (Gross National Product) more than doubled. But when the war was over, American leaders feared that the depression of the 1930s might return. To maintain its prosperity, America needed to sell its goods overseas. It also needed new opportunities abroad to invest its capital. American leaders argued the case for a world economic system based on free trade and equal opportunity. Revisionists maintain that equal opportunity in foreign trade was not possible at the end of the Second World War. America was bound to dominate because the American economy had not suffered. Economic domination would lead to political domination. For the revisionists, the Cold War developed because of Russia's refusal to play the game according to America's rules.

The final explanation for the Cold War is the post-revisionist. Post-revisionist historians see little point in blaming one side or the other. They argue that the Cold War developed because the United States and the Soviet Union had nothing in common. Their political beliefs – which shaped their vision of the post-war world – were exact opposites. They distrusted each other because they knew so little about each other. Before the war they had operated on the fringes of international politics. America had favoured a policy of isolation. The Soviet Union had, for the most part, been treated as an outcast. With the collapse of the old European order, America

3 Captured German troops make their way through the ruins of Stalingrad in 1943. In addition to their human losses during the war, the Russians lost 5 million houses, 1700 towns and 70,000 villages. 25 million people were homeless in the Soviet Union at the end of the war.

and Russia moved centre stage as the two great powers. They saw themselves as rival models for the rest of mankind.

Readers will judge for themselves which of these three explanations is the most convincing. A word of warning is required at the outset. The evidence presented on the pages which follow is based almost entirely on Western sources. Western historians have access to speeches made by Soviet politicians and to Soviet newspapers which sometimes explain Soviet policy. They have the records of their own governments which explain what was said at meetings with Soviet officials. They also have access to secondary accounts written by communist politicians with 'inside' information. The writings of Milovan Djilas and the memoirs of Nikita Khrushchev are cases in point. But Western historians do not have access to the records of the Soviet Communist Party or of the Soviet government. Until such time as these become freely available, much of what is written about Soviet foreign policy is speculation and educated guesswork.

COLD WAR WARRIORS

On 12 March 1947, President Truman went before the American Congress and delivered the following speech:

At the present moment in world history nearly every nation must choose between alternative ways of life. The choice is too often not a free one.

One way of life is based on the will of the majority, and is distinguished by free institutions, representatives government, free elections, guarantees of individual liberty, freedom of speech and religion, and freedom from political oppression.

The second way of life is based upon the will of a minority forcibly imposed upon the majority. It relies upon terror and oppression, a controlled press and radio, fixed elections, and the suppression of personal freedoms.

I believe that it must be the policy of the United States to support free peoples who are resisting attempted subjugation [subjection] by armed minorities or by outside pressures. (Royal Institute of International Affairs, *Documents on International Affairs 1947-48*)

4 The Truman Doctrine. President Truman delivers his speech to Congress, 12 March 1947.

Truman's speech persuaded the American Congress to vote in favour of supplying economic and military aid mainly to Greece but also to neighbouring Turkey. The government in Athens was fighting a civil war against the Greek communists. But the speech had much wider significance. It became known as the Truman Doctrine and it established a new American foreign policy known as containment. The aim was to contain the growth of communist influence and Soviet power. The methods by which this would be achieved developed in the years which followed. Economic and military aid was sent to countries threatened by communism. Alli-

ances, which gave the Americans military and naval bases in strategically important areas of the world, were then made with non-communist countries. If all else failed, America became directly involved. American troops were sent to Korea in the fifties and to Vietnam in the sixties.

The idea of containment lay behind another important step taken by the Americans in 1947. This was the Marshall Plan for a European economic recovery. George Marshall was the American Secretary of State between 1947 and 1949. In an important speech at Harvard in June 1947, Marshall announced that the American government was willing to provide dollars to enable the Europeans to rebuild their economies, which had yet to recover from the devastation of war. Economically, the Marshall Plan was designed to bring prosperity to Europe and continuing prosperity to the United States. A healthy Europe would become a major export area for American goods. But the Plan also had the political objective of containing communism. Unless the economies of Western Europe improved quickly, the voters might turn to the communists as the only political movement capable of ending the misery of unemployment, food rationing and fuel shortages. The danger seemed particularly serious in France and Italy. Both countries had large communist parties which commanded substantial support from the industrial workforce.

The Marshall Plan was intended to apply to the whole of Europe. The Russians seemed interested. Molotov, the Soviet foreign minister, led a delegation of over 80 Soviet economic specialists which arrived at Paris in July 1947 for a conference to discuss the details of the Marshall Plan. But serious differences soon arose between the Russians on the one hand and the British and French on the other. The British and French were not keen on Russian participation. The Russians for their part did not want foreigners prying into their internal affairs to find out how much aid the Soviet Union needed. Acting on Stalin's orders, Molotov walked out of the conference. Other East European countries – notably Poland and Czechoslovakia – were ordered to withdraw from the negotiations. The West Europeans alone reaped the benefits of the Marshall Plan.

Stalin drew his own conclusions about the Truman Doctrine and the Marshall Plan. He saw both as an American attempt to dominate Europe, both politically and economically. The Marshall Plan began to look sinister to the Russians. An economic recovery in Western Europe would lead to a military recovery. Backed by American atomic weapons, Western Europe would then be in a position to threaten Russian gains in Eastern Europe. Stalin responded by declaring his own version of the Cold War. The Soviet Union became a closed society. Abroad, the Cominform (Communist Information Bureau) was established to coordinate Soviet control of the major European communist parties. At the same time, non-communist politicians were eliminated from the governments of Eastern Europe. One by one, the countries of Eastern Europe became single-party communist dictatorships.

Nineteen forty-seven was the crucial year in the emergence of the Cold War. This chapter examines the influence of two individuals who played key roles. First, George Kennan, an American diplomat regarded by many as the author of the 'containment' policy. Secondly, Andrei Zhdanov, the man who was responsible for ideological affairs in the Soviet Union from the end of the war until his death in 1948.

5 George Marshall (left), the American Secretary of State and author of the Marshall Plan, with Vyacheslav Molotov, the Soviet foreign minister, at a conference in London, December 1947.

George Frost Kennan (1904-   )

George Kennan joined the American foreign service in 1926 and trained to become a Russian specialist. The United States established diplomatic relations with the Soviet Union in 1933 and an American embassy was opened in Moscow at the beginning of 1934. Kennan was one of the first American diplomats to be posted to the new embassy. It was a novel experience and Kennan enjoyed himself. The atmosphere in Moscow was quite open and relaxed. The Russians were good hosts.

But the honeymoon did not last long. Sergei Kirov, head of the Communist Party organization in Leningrad, was murdered in December 1934. Kirov's murder served as a warning. Stalin's purges and the great 'show' trials were about to begin. The atmosphere for the Americans changed. They were kept under close surveillance by the NKVD, Stalin's secret police.

Kennan spent many hours attempting to make sense of the purges and of Stalin's behaviour. Since the Bolshevik revolution of 1917, most Western governments had been trying to decide how far the communists had changed Russia. Kennan turned the question round by asking himself how far Russia had changed the communists:

After all, nations, like individuals, are largely the product of their environment; and many of their characteristics, their fears and their neuroses, as well as their abilities, are conditioned by the impressions of what we may call their early childhood. (George F. Kennan, *Memoirs 1925-50*)

Kennan saw many similarities between life in Russia under the Czars and life under Stalin. The rulers might have changed but the environment had not. Kennan studied Russian history and concluded that Russian rulers had always felt insecure. The country had no clearly defined frontiers and it had been invaded from both east and west on countless occasions throughout its history. This insecurity gave rise to a ruthless form of government based on personal despotism. Foreigners and foreign countries were always viewed as potential enemies, never as possible allies. Russian rulers governed with an iron hand and Western ideas about democratic rights had never taken root.

As well as feeling insecure, Kennan believed that the Russians had an inferiority complex. Economically, they had always lagged behind the West. In an attempt to close the gap and to modernize their country, Russian rulers from Peter the Great in the seventeenth century to Stalin in the twentieth had resorted to extreme methods. To Kennan, Stalin was the latest in a long line of Russian despots and communism in Russia was simply the old Russian despotism dressed up in a new form.

6 George Kennan, whose 'Long Telegram' shaped America's policy of containment.

From December 1941, America and Russia were allies in the war against Hitler. But Kennan's views remained unchanged. He still believed that the Russians were deeply suspicious of the outside world. When the war ended he was convinced that Stalin would never surrender the gains made by the Red Army. He was sure that Stalin would impose communist governments in those East European countries which had been occupied by the Red Army. They would be puppet governments, serving the cause not of communism but of Russian power. The West could do nothing because the Red Army was too strong. For the foreseeable future, the West would have to accept the division of Europe into spheres of Western and Soviet influence. Kennan was anxious that the West should not help the Russians, either by giving them aid to rebuild their economy or by recognizing Stalin's puppet governments in Eastern Europe.

Kennan's views were not shared by the American government. Few Americans could match Kennan's experience of the Soviet Union but the American government never asked him for his opinions. Franklin D. Roosevelt, America's wartime president, believed he could influence Stalin through personal diplomacy. Roosevelt died in April 1945. Harry Truman, the new president, was less sure of himself. He needed time to gain experience.

In Moscow, Kennan brooded in silence. He was convinced that he was right about the Russians and that his own government was wrong. But the situation changed at the beginning of 1946. Doubts were growing in Truman's mind. He believed that the Russians were going back on their word to arrange free elections in Eastern Europe. In February 1946 Stalin delivered an important speech in Moscow. He emphasized that Soviet communism, as well as the Red Army, had enabled Russia to defeat Hitler. The American government was puzzled. What did Stalin mean and did the speech give any clues about future Russian policy? The government decided to consult Kennan. Having been ignored for so long, this was Kennan's

7 Nikolai Bukharin (right) with Vyacheslav Molotov. Bukharin was one of the most famous victims of Stalin's purges. He was executed after a show trial in 1938. Kennan's views about the Soviet Union were formed during the period of the purges.

opportunity. 'They had asked for it', he wrote in his memoirs, 'Now, by God, they would have it.'

Kennan's reply took the form of a telegram which he sent to Washington in February 1946. It was about 8000 words in length and hence became known as the 'Long Telegram'. Kennan included his own views about Russian history, the Russian environment and the Russian character. Then he came to his main argument:

We have here a political force committed fanatically to the belief that with the United States there can be no permanent *modus vivendi* [compromise], that it is desirable and necessary that the internal harmony of our society be disrupted, our traditional way of life be destroyed, the international authority of our state be broken, if Soviet power is to be secure.

Kennan painted a frightening picture. But he also had a solution. Soviet power, he wrote, was not like that of Hitler's Germany:

It does not work by fixed plans. It does not take unnecessary risks. Impervious [unmoved] by the logic of reason, it is highly sensitive to the logic of force. For this reason it can easily withdraw – and usually does – when strong resistance is encountered at any point. Thus, if the adversary [opponent] has sufficient force and makes clear his readiness to use it, he rarely has to do so. (Kennan, *Memoirs*)

Kennan therefore argued that if the United States kept its nerve, remained alert and refused to be bullied, it would be possible to 'contain' Soviet power.

Kennan was not exaggerating when he later wrote that the effect produced by his telegram in Washington was 'nothing less than sensational'. Everyone in the administration read it, including President Truman. Kennan became a household name. His Long Telegram became the bible for American policymakers and containment became the American policy for dealing with the Soviet Union. The civil war in Greece, which led to the Truman Doctrine in 1947, was the first occasion upon which the policy was put into practice.

The name of George Kennan will always be linked with the policy of containment. It would be wrong to assume that the policy was entirely his creation but he was certainly a major influence. And yet Kennan was never happy with his reputation as the author of containment. He soon began to realise that Stalin was not a fanatical revolutionary but a cautious political leader faced with the daunting task of rebuilding the Soviet economy. In later years Kennan admitted that his Long Telegram had painted a distorted and exaggerated picture of Soviet communism.

Nor was Kennan happy with the manner in which American governments applied the policy of containment. Kennan did not want containment to become an open-ended commitment. If this happened, American resources would be stretched to the limit. Kennan had a limited view of containment which he explained in a series of talks and lectures in the late 1940s. He recalled what he said when he wrote his memoirs:

I expressed in talks and lectures the view that there were only five regions of the world – the United States, the United Kingdom, the Rhine valley with adjacent industrial areas, the Soviet Union, and Japan – where the sinews [mainstays] of modern military strength could be produced in quantity. I pointed out that only one of these was under communist control; and I defined the main task of containment, accordingly, as one of seeing to it that none of the remaining ones fell under such control.

But Kennan's limited view of containment was not shared by the American government. Truman and the presidents who came after him regarded the struggle against communism as a crusade. They believed that America had a moral duty to help any government, democratic or not, in any part of the world against the threat of communism. They took what became known as the 'domino theory' very seriously, namely the idea that if one country fell to communism, a chain reaction would be sparked in neighbouring countries. Beliefs such as these led the Americans into the tragedy of the Vietnam War.

Kennan left the foreign service in 1950. He continued to write and to lecture on the subject of American foreign policy. He was often critical but, as before, but nobody in the government listened to him.

8 British paratroopers in Greece during the civil war. When Britain pulled out in 1947, the Americans stepped in with economic and military aid. Greece was the first example of America's containment policy in action.

Andrei Zhdanov (1896-1948)

Andrei Zhdanov was Stalin's chief ideological spokesman when the war ended. It was his task to explain Soviet policies in Marxist-Leninist terms. At a time when Russian affairs were dominated by the cult of Stalin's personality, Zhdanov was one of those shadowy figures about whom little personally is known. One outsider who met him was Milovan Djilas, the Yugoslav communist. Djilas described Zhdanov as being 'rather short, with a brownish clipped moustache, a high forehead, pointed nose, and a sickly red face'.

As the chief ideologist, Zhdanov paid special attention to the arts in the Soviet Union at the end of the war. With Russia becoming a closed society, Zhdanov led a campaign in favour of 'Socialist Realism' in the arts. Socialist Realism imposed rigid limitations on people involved in the arts. They were not allowed to use their own imaginations or to express themselves freely. Instead, they had to conform to certain standards and requirements. Every novelist, artist and musician was expected to produce work describing the struggle for socialism in the Soviet Union. Stories about the heroic struggles of peasants toiling on collective farms, of workers labouring in factories and of soldiers defending the Fatherland during the Great Patriotic War [Second World War] were the only forms of acceptable popular literature. The state censors, working under Zhdanov's supervision, ensured that any hint of Western cultural influence was immediately suppressed.

Martin McCauley, a British historian, describes the impact of Zhdanov's campaign on the arts in the Soviet Union. He points out that science was affected in the same way and that life was made very difficult for the non-Russian nationalities of the Soviet Union:

Intellectually, the Soviet Union turned in on herself after the war, and foreign learning and achievements were scorned. The man who spearheaded this process was Andrei Zhdanov . . . . Literature was the first to be attacked. The journal *Leningrad* was closed down after being accused of publishing material which was 'permeated [saturated] with the spirit of servility towards everything foreign'. Then Zhdanov called Mikhail Zoshchenko, a leading satirist, the 'scum of the literary world' and declared that he could not decide whether Anna Akhmatova, a

9 Andrei Zhdanov, keeper of the Soviet Union's ideological keys both at home and abroad until his death in 1948.

leading poetess, was a nun or a whore. 'Kow-towing to the west', or praising anything foreign, was condemned . . . . The object of this exercise was not to convince writers, academics and scientists that Zhdanov's views – and by extension Stalin's – were correct, but to frighten them. It was an assault on the mind. Along with this went the glorification of all things Russian; anything worth discovering had been discovered by a Russian . . . . Russian nationalism became even more prominent than during the 1930s. It . . . heralded the downgrading of the achievements of the non-Russian nations in the USSR. One group of citizens who came in for much criticism because of the international situation were the Jews. Jewish theatres and journals were closed down and Jewish intellectuals were arrested. The years 1948-53 were black ones indeed for Soviet Jewry. (Martin McCauley, *Stalin and Stalinism*)

Zhdanov was also given the task of explaining Soviet foreign policy. He was the main Soviet speaker when the Cominform met for the first time in Poland in September 1947. The Cominform consisted of the Soviet Communist Party, the East European communist parties of Poland, Czechoslovakia, Hungary, Romania, Bulgaria and Yugoslavia, and the two West European Communist parties of France and Italy. The Cominform replaced the Comintern (Communist International), which had not met since 1935 and which had been disbanded in 1943. The Cominform had a smaller membership than the Comintern but it served the same purpose. It existed to ensure Soviet control over the communist parties in the countries concerned.

The first meeting of the Cominform was significant for two reasons. First, Zhdanov used the meeting to attack the Truman Doctrine and the Marshall Plan. Secondly, Zhdanov used the meeting to explain his theory that the international situation was now dominated by two rival camps.

Zhdanov argued that the Truman Doctrine and the Marshall Plan were both part of a single American policy towards Europe. The aim was to achieve American domination. In his speech to the Cominform, Zhdanov outlined what he saw as the main features of the Truman Doctrine:

1. Creation of American bases in the Eastern Mediterranean with the purpose of establishing American supremacy in that area.
2. Demonstrative support of the reactionary regimes in Greece and Turkey as bastions of American imperialism against the new democracies in the Balkans [Albania, Bulgaria, Romania and Yugoslavia].
3. Unremitting pressure on the countries of the new democracy, as expressed in false accusations of totalitarianism and expansionist ambitions, in attacks on the foundations of the new democratic regime, in constant interference in their domestic affairs . . . . (*Documents on International Affairs, 1947-48*)

On the Marshall Plan, Zhdanov had this to say

The vague and deliberately guarded formulations of the 'Marshall Plan', amount in essence to a scheme to create a bloc of states bound by obligations to the United States, and to grant American credits to European countries as a recompense [compensation] for their renunciation [surrender] of economic, and then of political, independence. Moreover, the cornerstone of the 'Marshall Plan' is the restoration of the industrial areas of West Germany controlled by the American monopolies.

In attacking the Marshall Plan, Zhdanov was especially critical of socialist parties in Western Europe. Clement Attlee, the British Labour prime minister, and Ernest Bevin, his foreign secretary, were said to be the agents of American imperialism because they welcomed the Marshall Plan. The same charge was levelled against Leon Blum and Paul Ramadier, the leaders of the French socialists. Zhdanov called for resistance to the Marshall Plan. He urged communists to take the lead:

In view of the fact that the majority of the socialist parties (especially the British Labourites and the French socialists) are acting as agents of the United States imperialist circles, there has devolved upon the Communists the special historical task of leading the resistance to the American plan . . . . The Communists must be the leaders in enlisting all anti-fascist and freedom-loving elements in the struggle against the new American expansionist plans for the enslavement of Europe.

The French and Italian parties were singled out because they were the biggest West European communist parties. Delegates from these two parties returned home with instructions to make the Marshall Plan unworkable by creating industrial unrest. A wave of strikes followed in France and Italy but the communists did not achieve their objective. In fact they became isolated because other political parties united against them.

At the end of the conference, the Cominform issued a statement on the international situation. The statement was the work of Zhdanov. Two rival camps were said to exist. They were led by the Soviet Union and the United States. Rivalry existed because the leaders and their allies emerged at the end of the war with different war aims:

10 Striking French miners at Lille demonstrating for a 25 per cent pay rise in December 1947. Acting on instructions from the Cominform, the French Communists organized strikes and lock-outs in an effort to sabotage the Marshall Plan and to bring down the French government.

The Soviet Union and the other democratic countries regarded as their basic war aims the restoration and consolidation of democratic order in Europe, the eradication of fascism and the prevention of the possibility of new aggression on the part of Germany, and the establishment of a lasting all-round co-operation among the nations of Europe. The United States of America, and Britain in agreement with them, set themselves another aim in the war: to rid themselves of competitors on the market (Germany and Japan) and to establish their dominant position . . . . Thus two camps were formed – the imperialist and anti-democratic camp having as its basic aim the establishment of world domination of American imperialism and the smashing of democracy, and the anti-imperialist and democratic camp having as its basic aim the undermining of imperialism, the consolidation of democracy, and the eradication of the remnant of fascism.

Zhdanov's speech and the Cominform's statement represented the Russian reply to the Truman Doctrine and the Marshall Plan. The language used was just as dramatic and extreme as that used by President Truman in his speech to Congress. The Cold War had been declared on both sides. It was as much a war of words as it was a war of deeds. Zhdanov had made a crucial contribution to the language of the Cold War.

EASTERN EUROPE

No longer prime minister but still an influential voice as leader of the opposition in Britain, Winston Churchill travelled to the United States in 1946 and delivered an important speech at Fulton, Missouri, on 5 March. 'It is my duty', he told his audience, 'to place before you certain facts about the present position in Europe'. He went on:

Nobody knows what Soviet Russia and its Communist international organization intends to do in the immediate future, or what are the limits, if any, to their expansive . . . tendencies . . . .

From Stettin in the Baltic to Trieste in the Adriatic an iron curtain has descended across the Continent . . . . The Communist parties, which were very small in all these eastern states of Europe, have been raised to pre-eminence far beyond their numbers and are seeking everywhere to obtain totalitarian control . . . .

Whatever conclusions may be drawn from these facts – and facts they are – this is certainly not the liberated Europe we fought to build up. Nor is it one that contains the essentials of permanent peace . . . .

On the other hand . . . I repulse [reject] the idea that a new war is inevitable; still more that it is imminent . . . I do not believe that Soviet Russia desires war. What they desire is the fruits of war and the indefinite expansion of their power and doctrines . . . . (Royal Institute of International Affairs, *America, Britain and Russia 1941-46*)

Churchill's speech made the 'iron curtain' a familiar phrase. Orthodox historians of the Cold War claim that Churchill was quite right to sound the alarm bells about the communist threat in his Fulton speech. They argue that Stalin had a master-plan for the control of Eastern Europe. At first he allowed coalition governments to be set up but the non-communists were deliberately squeezed out. The communists always held the key positions in government, particularly the ministry of the interior, which gave them control over the police. They also controlled the ministries of broadcasting, education and information. Elections, when held, were not democratic. The votes were rigged. Stalin's plans, according to the orthodox historians, did not stop at Eastern Europe. If the opportunity presented itself, he intended to expand further west. It was this possibility that Churchill warned against in his Fulton speech.

Revisionist historians disagree. They deny that Stalin had a master-plan for Russian control in Eastern Europe because conditions varied from country to country. They argue that he wanted 'friendly' governments but not necessarily communist governments. Many revisionists also see Finland as the model of what Stalin wanted in Eastern Europe at the end of the war. Russia went to war with Finland in 1939 and the Finns were treated as a defeated enemy in 1945.

But Stalin made no attempt to impose a communist government. Instead, he reached agreement with J.K. Paasikivi, a conservative politician and Finland's first post-war prime minister. In April 1948, a Soviet-Finnish Mutual Assistance Pact was signed at Moscow. Under the terms of the Pact, the Finns pledged that they would never join an anti-Soviet alliance. By accepting this limitation on their defence and foreign policies, the Finns were able to keep their internal independence. But the Finnish model was not extended across Eastern Europe. Instead, in 1947-48, communist governments took power. The reason, according to the revisionists, was the change in American policy. Stalin's hand was forced by the

Truman Doctrine and the Marshall Plan.

This chapter examines what happened in three East European countries through the experiences of four politicians. First, Stanislaw Mikolajczyk, the deputy prime minister and minister of agriculture in Poland's first post-war government. Secondly, Eduard Beneš and Jan Masaryk, the President and foreign minister of Czechoslovakia. Finally, Milovan Djilas, Tito's right-hand man in Yugoslavia. Djilas made a number of visits to Moscow which gave him a unique insight into the way Stalin's mind worked.

11 'Beware the Bogey Man'. Cartoon from the *Daily Mail*, 13 March 1946, depicting Stalin's reaction to Churchill's 'iron curtain' speech, at Fulton. In his reply to Churchill's speech, Stalin pointed out that the Soviet Union's loss of life during the war had been several times greater than that of America and Britain put together. It was therefore not surprising, he said, that the Soviet Union should want 'loyal' governments in those East European states recently liberated from Germany.

12 Map of Europe showing the line of the 'iron curtain'.

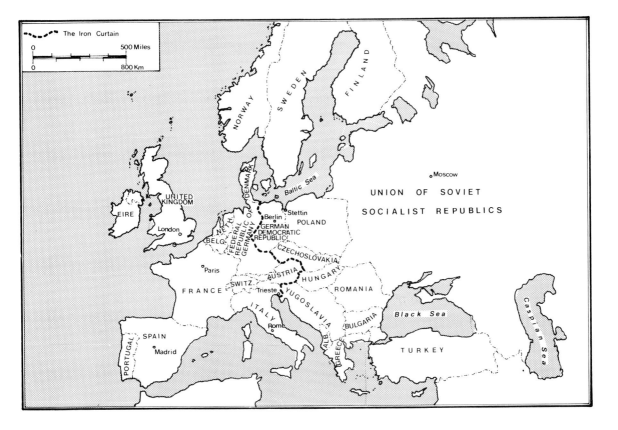

Stanislaw Mikolajczyk (1901-1966)

In September 1939, when Poland was invaded first by Germany and then by the Soviet Union, the leaders of the government in Warsaw moved to Paris. In June 1940, when France surrendered to Germany, the Polish leaders moved to Britain. In London they established a Polish government-in-exile under General Sikorski. When Sikorski died in 1943 he was succeeded by Stanislaw Mikolajczyk.

The purpose of the government-in-exile was to keep alive the spirit of Poland's independence and to win international recognition. America and Britain recognized the government immediately. The Russians did likewise in July 1941, a month after the German invasion of the Soviet Union. But the Polish government-in-exile never trusted the Russians. The Russian occupation of eastern Poland between 1939 and 1941 under the Nazi-Soviet pact was still fresh in the memory.

Relations between the London Poles and Stalin worsened in April 1943 when the Germans announced the discovery of a mass grave near the village of Katyn in the district of Smolensk in eastern Poland. The grave contained the bodies of over 4000 Polish army officers. The Russians strongly denied the German accusation that 'the Bolsheviks' had been responsible for the massacre. Mikolajczyk and the London Poles demanded an enquiry by the International Red Cross. Stalin reacted angrily by breaking off diplomatic relations with the Poles in London.

The Katyn discovery isolated Mikolajczyk and his colleagues in London. They wanted American and British support for an enquiry but Roosevelt and Churchill were anxious to let the matter drop. With the war entering a crucial phase, the Americans and British could not afford to offend their Russian ally.

Worse followed for the London Poles. At the Tehran conference in November 1943, Roosevelt, Churchill and Stalin made some important decisions about the frontiers of a post-war Polish state. It was agreed that the Soviet Union would annex the eastern territories of Poland up to a line (the Curzon line) which had been drawn in 1920. Poland would be compensated by taking over territory from Germany in the west up to the rivers Oder and Neisse. Mikolajczyk was not consulted. When he was told about the agreements by Churchill, he refused to accept them. For the London Poles, the Tehran agreements represented yet another in a long line of partitions of Poland which had been imposed by the great powers.

But there was little that Mikolajczyk could do to influence what was happening. In July 1944, with the Red Army already on Polish soil, the Russians established a Committee of National Liberation in the town of Lublin. The Lublin Committee was manned by Polish communists. Stalin insisted that the Committee should form the basis of a new Polish government at the end of the war. Inside Poland, non-communists tried to stop this happening. Between July and October 1944, the leaders of the Home Army (the Polish resistance) in Warsaw launched an armed uprising against the city's German occupiers. They wanted to liberate Warsaw before the Red Army arrived. Aware of their motive, Stalin refused to help the Home Army until it was too late. The Home Army had to surrender and Hitler gave instructions that Warsaw should be razed to the ground.

Towards the end of the uprising, Mikolajczyk flew from London to Moscow for talks about Poland's future. Churchill and Anthony Eden, the British foreign secretary, were also present. Mikolajczyk carried with him the final terms which the London Poles were prepared to offer for an agreement about Poland's government and frontiers at the end of the war. They wanted the Polish communists to have no more than one-fifth of the seats in the new government and they insisted that certain districts in eastern Poland should not be handed over to the Soviet Union. The Moscow meeting was the scene of a furious argument between Mikolajczyk and Churchill. Stalin said nothing; he had no need to. Neal Ascherson, a British journalist and a specialist on Poland's history, recalls what happened at the meeting:

Deeply shaken, Mikolajczyk now met Churchill and Eden in private. Churchill reproached him: if he had only agreed to the Curzon Line frontier earlier in the year, Stalin would not have set up a rival 'government' in the form of the Lublin Committee . . . Mikolajczyk bitterly reminded him of Britain's pledges to Poland. Churchill shouted at him that he wanted to start a third world war. 'You're a callous people who want to wreck Europe. I shall leave you to your own troubles. You have only your miserable, petty, selfish interests in mind.'

He [Churchill] threatened to withdraw recognition of the London government, and added that Mikolajczyk ought to be in a lunatic asylum. Beside himself with rage and misery, Mikolajczyk demanded permission to be parachuted into Poland, so he could perish in battle with the [Home] Army . . . .

At this Churchill marched out of the room. Both men were close to tears. After some moments Churchill returned and put his arms around the Pole's shoulders. But they had reached the end of the line, and they knew it . . . .

Mikolajczyk went back to London. There he told his colleagues . . . that there was no longer any room for manoeuvre. If they wanted to have any share of the future government, they would have to swallow the Soviet terms and the Curzon Line. He urged them to do so, reminding them of the rich new territories promised to Poland in the west. But it was too much for most of the London Poles, and on 24 November Mikolajczyk resigned.

This was the end of the Polish exile government as a force in international politics. From now on, world statesmen acted as if it no longer existed. (Neal Ascherson, *The Struggles for Poland*)

The Tehran agreement about Poland's frontiers was confirmed when the great powers met at Yalta in February 1945. But Mikolajczyk was not yet finished. He returned to Poland at the end of the war and became one of two deputy prime ministers in a new provisional government. He was also minister of agriculture and leader of the Polish Peasant Party, which drew its support from Poland's farmers. The government was dominated by members of the Lublin Com-mittee – they held 16 of the 25 seats. Real power rested with Wladislaw Gomulka, the other deputy prime minister, who was also secretary of the Polish United Worker's or Communist Party.

For the first year the new government held together. The communists behaved with caution. They knew that they did not have widespread support because of their close association with the Russians. The first test of public opinion came in June 1946. A referendum was held in which the Polish people were asked to support government policy on three issues: the abolition of the Senate (the upper

13 Stanislaw Mikolajczyk, leader of the London Poles and the Polish Peasant Party at the end of the war. He fled Poland in 1947.

14 German troops survey the mass grave containing the bodies of some 4000 Polish officers at Katyn in 1943. It is only now, with Gorbachev in power in the Soviet Union, that the Russians are prepared to admit their responsibility for the murders. This photograph was published by the Nazis in France – hence the French caption.

house of the Polish parliament), economic reform (changes in land ownership and nationalization), and acceptance of Poland's new frontiers in the west.

Mikolajczyk supported government policy on all three issues. But to demonstrate his independence he called upon his supporters to vote 'no' on the first. He lost. The official result announced that 68 per cent had voted in favour of abolishing the Senate and only 32 per cent against. But the result did not reflect the true position. Jerry Morawski, one of the younger communist leaders at the end of the war, later admitted that the result had been fixed:

I found out afterwards that the results had been faked. In reality, the situation was probably just the reverse: two-thirds had voted for what Mikolajczyk was asking. (Ascherson, *Struggles*)

The referendum came as a shock to the communists. As Morawski recalled:

It was a warning which showed how strong the influence of Mikolajczyk's opposition was in Poland. It showed how much effort to pressurize, destroy, intimidate and discredit Mikolajczyk's opposition was still needed in order to win the elections. (Ascherson, *Struggles*)

Elections for a new government, which had been postponed on several occasions, were eventually held in January 1947. As polling day drew nearer, the Peasant Party was subjected to a campaign of official terror. Their meetings were disrupted, their members arrested and their buildings attacked. Mikolajczyk was now a lonely figure. The policies of the Western powers did not help him. America's policy of containment suggested that the West had abandoned Poland. Containment was designed to isolate communism in Eastern Europe, not to rescue individual East European countries from the threat of communism. The Western powers also voiced their opposition to Poland's western frontier. The Oder-Neisse line, they

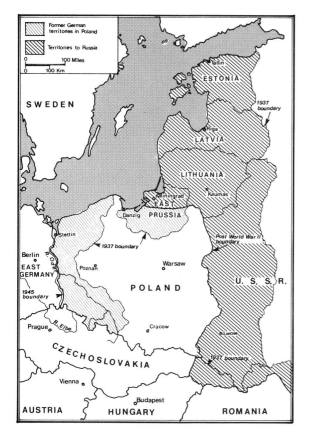

said, had been imposed by the Russians.

Statements such as this served only to strengthen the position of the communists in Poland. As in the case of the referendum, the elections of 1947 were rigged. They were won by the Democratic Bloc, a group of left-wing parties dominated by the communists. The Democratic Bloc had 394 seats in the new parliament. The Peasant Party had only 28. The West protested but did nothing. Stalin ignored the protests.

Mikolajczyk was now powerless. Moreover, as the Russians tightened their grip on Eastern Europe in the autumn of 1947, Mikolajczyk realized that his life was in danger. In 1947 he was smuggled to the coast in an American embassy car and put on board a ship for the west. He arrived in Britain but then moved to the United States, where he died 19 years later.

15 Map of Poland showing the territories lost to the Soviet Union and those gained from Germany at the end of the war.

16 German troops rounding up the Poles who surrendered at the end of the Warsaw Uprising in 1944.

Eduard Beneš (1884-1948) and Jan Masaryk (1886-1948)

Born into a peasant family in Bohemia, Eduard Beneš was a Czechoslovak nationalist. Together with Tomas Masaryk, the first president of Czechoslovakia, Beneš led the movement for an independent Czechoslovak state, which came into being in 1918 at the end of the First World War. Beneš was foreign minister of Czechoslovakia between 1918 and 1935 and became president in 1935 when Masaryk retired. Jan Masaryk was the son of Tomas Masaryk. He began a diplomatic career at the end of the First World War. He was a member of the Czechoslovak delegation to the Paris Peace Conference of 1919-20. Between 1925 and 1935 he represented his country as a diplomat in London.

Beneš resigned the presidency in 1938 because of the Munich Agreement. Jan Masaryk followed his example by resigning from the diplomatic service. At Munich in 1938, the heads of government of Germany, Britain, France and Italy reached agreement that the Sudetenland should be transferred to Germany. A fortified region on the border with Germany, the Sudetenland was part of Czechoslovakia. It had never been part of Germany but it was inhabited by a German-speaking minority. Hitler threatened war over the Sudetenland and no Czechoslovak representative was present at Munich. Czechoslovakia ceased to be an independent state in March 1939 when Hitler sent his troops into Prague.

A Czechoslovak government-in-exile was established in London in 1940. It was led by Beneš. Jan Masaryk became foreign minister and deputy prime minister. Both men returned to Prague at the end of the war. Beneš became president again; Masaryk continued as foreign minister.

During and immediately after the war, Czechoslovakia's foreign policy continued to be influenced by the 1938 Munich Agreement.

Munich made Beneš and Masaryk realize that they could not depend on the Western powers alone to defend Czechoslovakia. Both men wanted Czechoslovakia to act as a bridge-builder between East and West and between communism and democracy. To achieve this, they had to develop friendly relations with the Soviet Union. Beneš travelled to Moscow in December 1943 and signed a Russo-Czech Treaty of Friendship, Alliance and Mutual Assistance. At Moscow, Beneš had discussions with Stalin and Klement Gottwald, the leader of the Czech communists. Agreement was reached that the communists should play a major role in the

17 Eduard Beneš, president of Czechoslovakia at the time of the communist takeover in February 1948.

post-war government of Czechoslovakia. The communists achieved this when they won 38 per cent of the vote in elections which were held in April 1946. With only nine of the 27 seats, the communists were in a minority in the new cabinet. But Gottwald was appointed prime minister and the communists also controlled the key ministries of the interior and information.

Beneš and Masaryk realized that they could not afford to offend the Soviet Union. They accepted that they did not have a free hand in foreign policy. Account had to be taken of Czechoslovakia's geographical position and Russia's military power. Petr Zenkl, another non-communist Czech politician, explained the reasoning behind the Beneš-Masaryk policy:

We know that the freedom of action of every small country is nowadays to a certain extent limited, and we know this is doubly true about a country in our geographical position. Accepting this limitation, we do so nevertheless in the spirit of Masaryk and Beneš, namely above all in the interest of international understanding which, as is known, demands a certain limitation of sovereignty [independence] of every state. (Martin McCauley [ed], *Communist Power in Europe 1944-49*)

However, the Beneš-Masaryk policy met with disapproval in both Washington and London. The American and British governments believed that Beneš and Masaryk were playing into the hands of the communists. The Americans in particular were not impressed by Masaryk. James Riddleberger, a State Department official, wrote to Laurence Steinhardt, the American Ambassador in Prague:

I share your feelings of disappointment in this man [Masaryk] who might well have utilized his background and name to stand up to the communist extremists on behalf of the pro-Western elements and seriously attempted to influence the Government toward a course that

18 Jan Masaryk, the Czech foreign minister whose death in March 1948 shocked the West.

would not alienate the Soviet Union yet at the same time preserve the friendly regard of the United States. I judge that he has either been weak or blind. (Yergin, *Shattered Peace*)

The Americans showed little sympathy or understanding for the position of Beneš and Masaryk. In fact, American policy towards Czechoslovakia served only to increase their difficulties. The summer harvest of 1947 in Czechoslovakia was very poor. Grain and potato production reached only 63 per cent and 48 per cent of their respective targets. Masaryk appealed to the United States for food and loans but Washington refused unless Czechoslovakia changed its foreign policy. The Russians stepped in with a promise of 600,000 tons of grain. Hubert Ripka, one of Masaryk's deputies responsible for foreign trade, commented bitterly:

Those goddam Americans. We . . . asked for 200,000 or 300,000 tons of wheat. And those idiots started the usual blackmail . . . . At that point Gottwald got in touch with Stalin, who promised us the required wheat. And now those idiots in Washington have driven us straight into the Stalinist camp . . . . The fact that not America but Russia had saved us from starvation will have a tremendous effect inside Czechoslovakia – even among the people whose sympathies are with the West rather than Moscow. (Yergin, *Shattered Peace*)

American policy had the effect of isolating the non-communists in the Czech government. From the autumn of 1947, these same politicians found themselves under increasing pressure from the communists. With the creation of the Cominform, the Czechs were not allowed to participate in the discussions about the Marshall Plan. The Americans were already beginning to write Czechoslovakia off. In November 1947, in a top-secret briefing, George Marshall informed Truman's cabinet:

The halt in the communist advance is forcing Moscow to consolidate its hold on Eastern Europe. It will probably have to clamp down completely on Czechoslovakia, for a relatively

free Czechoslovakia . . . could too easily become a means of entry of really democratic forces into Eastern Europe in general . . . . It is purely a defensive move. (Yergin, *Shattered Peace*)

Marshall might have added that Stalin could not afford to let Czechoslovakia slip. The country was the Soviet Union's most important source of uranium – an essential commodity in the production of atomic weapons.

The growing political crisis in Czechoslovakia reached its climax in February 1948. Increasingly isolated and without adequate support from the West, the non-communist politicians in the Czech government gambled – and lost. On 20 February, the day after the arrival in Prague of Valerian Zorin, the Soviet deputy foreign minister, 12 non-communist politicians of the government (Masaryk was not one of them) handed their resignations to President Beneš. They thought they had an understanding with Beneš that he would not accept them. Instead, they expected that Beneš would either form a new cabinet (with fewer communist members) or that he would call for new elections much earlier than the planned date of May.

But Beneš was now a sick man. He had suffered a stroke the previous summer and he had not fully recovered. He was also haunted by the memory of the Munich Agreement and this perhaps explained why he hesitated. The communists quickly exploited the crisis. They formed Action Committees to take over the vacant ministries and they used the police to arrest and intimidate opponents. Eventually, on 25 February, Beneš gave way to communist pressure by allowing Gottwald to form a communist-dominated government.

Beneš stayed on as president but resigned in June 1948. He died, a broken man, three months later. Masaryk also stayed on as foreign minister but a few days later (on 10 March) he was killed in a fall from the window of the Foreign Ministry in Prague. Whether his death was murder or suicide has always been a mystery, but it is now widely believed that he took his own life.

Milovan Djilas (1911-   )

Milovan Djilas joined the Yugoslav Communist Party in 1932. Yugoslavia was then a monarchy and the communists had been banned. Djilas was arrested, tortured and imprisoned for three years. When Germany invaded Yugoslavia in 1941, the king fled and the country was divided between Germany and her allies – Italy, Bulgaria and Hungary. Under the leadership of Josip Broz, better known by his codename Tito, the Yugoslav communists retreated to the mountain regions of Yugoslavia where they organized a resistance movement. They were known as the Partisans. Djilas became one of Tito's Partisan generals. The Partisans waged a successful guerrilla war against the German invaders. Russian troops entered Yugoslavia in 1944 but the country was never occupied by the Red Army. The Partisans were largely responsible for Yugoslavia's liberation.

In 1944 Djilas led a Partisan military mission to Moscow. The Partisans wanted Russian loans. They also wanted to find out whether Stalin would recognize them as the legal government of Yugoslavia once the war was over. When he arrived, Djilas was asked to write articles about Tito and the struggle in Yugoslavia. His articles were heavily edited by the Russians. All references to Tito's personal contribution to the war effort and to the originality of his ideas were either taken out or watered down. Djilas was surprised:

For me and for other Yugoslav Communists Stalin's leadership was indisputable. Yet I was still puzzled why other Communist leaders – Tito, for instance – could not be praised if they deserved it, from the Communist point of view. (Milovan Djilas, *Conversations with Stalin*)

The incident over the articles was soon forgotten. After weeks of waiting, Djilas was told that a meeting had been arranged with Stalin. He was both nervous and excited:

What could be more exciting for a Communist, one who was coming from war and revolution, than to be received by Stalin? This was the greatest possible recognition of the heroism and suffering of our Partisan fighters and our people . . . Stalin was something more than a leader in battle. He was the incarnation [living symbol] of an idea . . . something infallible and sinless. Stalin was the victorious battle of today and the brotherhood of man of tomorrow. I realized that it was by chance that I personally was the first Yugoslav Communist to be received by him. Still, I felt a proud joy that I would be able tell my comrades about this encounter and say something about it to the Yugoslav fighting men as well. (Djilas, *Conversations*)

19 Milovan Djilas, Tito's special emissary to Stalin. Djilas fell out with Tito in the 1950s and was imprisoned.

Djilas had two meetings with Stalin during his 1944 visit. The first took place in the Kremlin. Stalin agreed to the loan and also said that ships would be provided to transport military and medical supplies to the Partisans in Yugoslavia. The ships never arrived. The second took place at Stalin's country house about 20 miles outside Moscow. Here Djilas was entertained to one of Stalin's famous dinner parties, which usually lasted six or more hours – from ten at night to four or five in the morning. Vast quantities of food and alcohol were consumed.

Djilas was not a heavy drinker and he found this second meeting something of an endurance test. The question of recognizing the Partisans as the legal government cropped up during the rambling discussions. Stalin advised caution. He did not want to give his allies, particularly the British, the impression that the communists were bidding for power in Yugoslavia.

Djilas came away from Moscow content with what had been achieved. He went back for a second visit in April 1945. By this time a provisional government had been established in Yugoslavia which was effectively controlled by the communists. Djilas returned to Moscow as a member of a delegation which was led by Tito. A Soviet-Yugoslav treaty of mutual assistance was signed. During a discussion of the war situation, Stalin told his visitors:

This war is not as in the past; whoever occupies a territory also imposes on it his own social system. Everyone imposes his own system as far as his army has power to do so. It cannot be otherwise. (Djilas, *Conversations*)

But the second visit to Moscow was not a success. Djilas knew before he went that he had made himself unpopular with the Russians. The Red Army entered north-east Yugoslavia in the autumn of 1944. Almost immediately, the Partisans began to receive complaints about the behaviour of Russian soldiers. They were said to be looting and to be guilty in over one hundred cases of rape. When Djilas raised the matter with Russian

officers he was himself accused of insulting the Red Army. Stalin was informed of the incident and made no secret of his displeasure when the Yugoslav delegation arrived in Moscow. At first he ignored Djilas. Then, when the incident came up in conversation, Stalin offered his own explanation:

Well then, imagine a man who has fought from Stalingrad to Belgrade – over thousands of kilometres of his own devastated land, across dead bodies of his comrades and dearest ones! How can such a man react normally? And what is so awful in his amusing himself with a woman, after such horrors? (Djilas, *Conversations*)

The visit was awkward in other ways. The Russians made jokes about the Yugoslav army which the Yugoslavs did not find funny. Stalin seemed reluctant to give the Yugoslavs credit for anything. He refused to accept that the Partisans had created a revolutionary situation in Yugoslavia. It was also apparent to Djilas that Stalin and Tito did not get on with each other. There were unmistakeable signs of tension:

One could detect in the relation between Stalin and Tito something special . . . as though these two had a grudge against one another, but each was holding back for his own reasons. Stalin took care not to offend Tito personally in any way, but at the same time he kept making underhand digs about the situation in Yugoslavia. On the other hand, Tito treated Stalin with respect, as one would one's senior, but resentment could also be detected, especially about Stalin's remarks about Yugoslavia. (Djilas, *Conversations*)

Djilas made a third and final visit to Moscow at the beginning of 1948 as a member of another Yugoslav delegation. A delegation representing the ruling communists of Bulgaria was also present. The Yugoslav and Bulgarian delegations had been summoned by the Soviet government to explain what was happening in the Balkans. The Yugoslavs and the Bulgarians wanted to create a Balkan federation at the end of the war. To aid their post-war recovery, they wanted to co-operate on economic matters by forming a customs union. As well as co-operating with each other, they wanted to include their neighbours.

Agreement had been reached in principle that Albania should form a federation with Yugoslavia. Bulgaria wanted to form a customs union with Romania. The Russians, as Djilas discovered during his 1948 visit, objected. Stalin accused the Yugoslavs of wanting to 'swallow' Albania. Kardelj, another member of the Yugoslav delegation, was called upon to explain why the Yugoslav government had sent troops into Albania. Djilas recalled the conversation:

Kardelj replied that we had the consent of the Albanian Government.

Stalin shouted, 'This could lead to serious international complications. Albania is an

20 Three faces of Tito, the nationalist leader of communist Yugoslavia. From the left, in 1927 when he was arrested because of his communist activities; in 1948 when Yugoslavia was expelled from the Cominform; and in 1971. Tito died in May 1980.

independent state. What do you think? Justification or no justification, the fact remains that you did not consult us about sending two divisions into Albania.'

Kardelj explained that none of this was final and added that he did not remember a single foreign problem about which the Yugoslav government had not consulted the Soviet Union.

'It's not so,' Stalin cried. 'You don't consult at all. That is not your mistake, but your policy – yes, your policy!'

Kardelj, cut short, fell silent and did not press his view. (Djilas, *Conversations*)

Dimitrov, leader of the Bulgarian delegation, received similar treatment. Why, he was asked, had there been no consultation about the customs union with Romania?:

Dimitrov . . . 'There are essentially no differences between the foreign policies of Bulgaria and the Soviet Union.'

Stalin . . . 'There are serious differences. Why hide it? It was Lenin's practice always to recognize errors and to remove them as quickly as possible.'

Dimitrov . . . 'True we erred. But through errors we are learning our way in foreign politics.'
Stalin . . . 'Learning! You have been in politics 50 years – and now you are correcting errors. Your trouble is not errors, but that you are taking a different line from ours.' (Djilas, *Conversations*)

For Djilas, the truth now dawned:

At that moment the point of the meeting suddenly became clear, though no one expressed it, namely that no relations between the 'people's democracies' were permissible that were not in the interests and had not the approval of the Soviet government . . . Stalin sought an arrangement of the East European countries that would strengthen and secure Moscow's domination . . . for a long time to come. (Djilas, *Conversations*)

The Yugoslavs were also criticized because they were supporting the communists who were fighting the civil war in Greece. Stalin shouted at his visitors:

What, do you think that Great Britain and the United States – the United States, the most powerful state in the world – will permit you to break their line of communication in the Mediterranean? Nonsense. And we have no navy. The uprising in Greece must be stopped, and as quickly as possible. (Djilas, *Conversations*)

Djilas began to realize where Stalin stood on the question of revolutions. He commented later:

Because Moscow had always refrained at the crucial moment from supporting the Chinese, the Spanish, and in many ways even the Yugoslav revolutions, the view prevailed, not without reason, that Stalin was generally against revolutions. This, however, is not entirely correct. His opposition was only conditional, and arose only when the revolution went beyond the interests of the Soviet state. He felt instinctively that the creation of revolutionary centres outside Moscow could endanger its supremacy in world communism. That is why he helped revolutions only up to a certain point – as long as he could control them – but he was always ready to leave them in the lurch whenever they slipped out of his grasp. (Djilas, *Conversations*)

At the end of his third visit, Djilas left Moscow a disappointed and disillusioned man. 'It was hard to believe', he later wrote, 'that I was the same person who four years earlier had eagerly travelled to the Soviet Union with an open heart and a disciple's devotion.' Plans to establish a Balkan federation were dropped but the Yugoslavs remained determined to keep their independence. In June 1948 the Yugoslav Communist Party was expelled from the Cominform.

THE DIVISION OF GERMANY

Whoever controls Berlin controls Germany, whoever controls Germany controls Europe.

This was how Lenin once described the importance of Germany. Hitler's Reich was the greatest prize for the victorious allies. From 1943 they agreed that they would not bargain or negotiate with Germany to bring the war to an end. Germany, they insisted, must surrender unconditionally.

At Yalta in February 1945 the allies agreed that Germany should be divided into zones of American, British and Soviet occupation. These three zones were later extended to four when a French zone was created out of the American and British zones. Berlin, the German capital, located 100 miles inside the Soviet zone, would likewise be divided into four allied sectors. Each occupying power would be responsible for the administration of its own zone. To co-ordinate policies for the whole country, an Allied Control Council would be established in Berlin.

The future of Germany was discussed again at the Potsdam conference in the summer of 1945. The allies confirmed the agreements reached at Yalta about Germany's eastern frontier. Poland would be allowed to administer territory which lay to the east of the Oder-Neisse line. But the final location of the frontier was left undecided. The details would be drawn up in a German peace treaty. It was also agreed at Potsdam that Germany should pay reparations. A precise sum was not mentioned but a formula for the payment of reparations was worked out. Each occupying power would take reparations from its own zone. Because they had suffered far more during the war, the Russians would be entitled to 10 per cent of all reparations taken from the Western zones. The Russians would also receive a further 15 per cent from the Western zones in return for food and raw materials from their own Eastern zone.

The idea of making the division of Germany permanent was not discussed at Potsdam. The agreement signed by the allies made it clear that Germany was to be treated as a single economic unit. It also declared: 'So far as is practicable, there shall be uniformity of treatment of the German population throughout Germany.' The aim therefore was to create a 'safe' Germany through demilitarization, denazification and democratization. A German peace treaty would then follow. But a treaty has never been signed. Four years after Potsdam two new German states were established – the Federal Republic of West Germany and the Democratic Republic of East Germay. The division of Germany in 1949 completed the Cold War division of Europe into Western and Eastern blocs. How and why did this happen?

In the months after Potsdam the idea of treating Germany as an economic unit broke down over the issue of reparations. At first the Americans blamed the French as much as the Russians. But then, as events unfolded in Eastern Europe, the United States and Britain began to see their own zones in Germany as an essential part of Western Europe's defence against communism. Steps were taken to merge the three western zones, both economically and politically. Stalin had no wish to see a powerful West Germany rise from the ashes of World War II. He made a last ditch effort to prevent what was happening in the Western zones by mounting a blockade of West Berlin in 1948.

But the blockade failed. The Western powers jumped over it, quite literally, by organizing an airlift. The blockade led directly

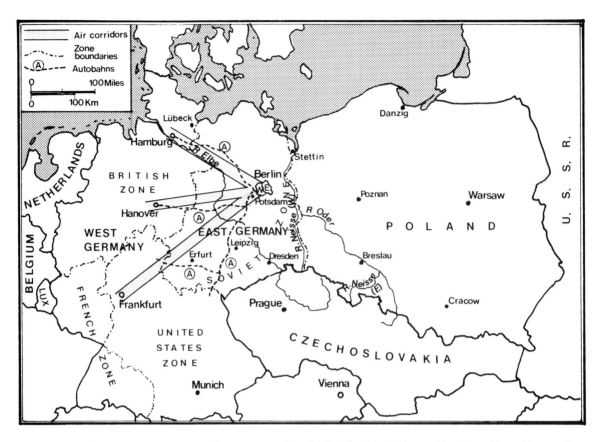

21 Map of Germany showing the four zones of occupation and the autobahn routes and air-corridors between the Western zones and Berlin.

to the division of Germany. It also led to the North Atlantic Treaty, which was signed in April 1949, a month before the blockade of West Berlin was lifted. The Treaty was signed by the United States, Canada, Britain, France, the Netherlands, Belgium, Luxembourg, Iceland, Norway, Italy and Portugal. Article 5 of the treaty declared that an attack on one of these states would be treated as an attack on them all. Never before in peacetime had the United States entered into such a commitment. Stalin was now confronted not only by a West German state but also by an indefinite American military presence in Europe. Ironically, Russian actions in Germany had produced the very results that Stalin was most anxious to avoid.

This chapter examines the division of Germany, and the consequences which followed, through the experiences of three individuals. First, Lucius D. Clay, the American military governor in Germany at the time of the Berlin blockade. Secondly, Konrad Adenauer, a conservative politician from the Western zones who became the first chancellor of West Germany in 1949. Finally, Walter Ulbricht, the leader of the communists in East Germany.

22 Berlin, the German capital, in ruins at the end of the war.

Lucius D. Clay (1897-1978)

Born in Georgia, the son of an American Senator, Lucius D. Clay graduated from West Point, the American military academy, in 1918. He distinguished himself as an engineer and administrator as he rose through the ranks. As the military governor in charge of the American zone of Germany at the end of the war, Clay was very jealous of his authority. His powers were extensive. A contemporary described the role of the military governor:

Military Governor was a pretty heady job. It was the nearest thing to a Roman proconsulship the modern world afforded. You could turn to your secretary and say, 'Take a law'. The law was there, and you could see its effect in two or three weeks. It was a challenging job to an ambitious man. Benevolent despotism. (Yergin, *Shattered Peace*)

During the first year of the occupation, Clay believed that he was making progress in co-operating with the Russians. He blamed the French for the difficulties which arose and he was very critical of the arguments put forward by Kennan in his Long Telegram. But by the end of 1946 Clay's early optimism about the Russians had faded. He was worn down by the never-ending problems which arose in negotiation with Marshal Sokolovsky, his Soviet opposite number on the Control Council. More significantly, the build-up of East-West tensions outside Germany convinced Clay that the Russians were concealing aggressive intentions.

Reparations were the first major stumbling block in treating Germany as an economic unit. In May 1946 Clay ordered a halt to the delivery of reparations from the American zone. His action was directed against the French as well as the Russians. Both seemed determined to bleed their own zones white. Russian actions particularly angered him. In the Eastern zone, the Russians began by dismantling entire factories. The parts were loaded on to trains and then reassembled when they arrived in the Soviet Union.

At the beginning of 1946, Russian policy changed. The factories were left intact but the goods produced were sent back to the Soviet Union. Meanwhile, in the American zone, serious food shortages began to develop. Like the British zone, the American zone in Germany was largely industrial. Both zones depended for their food on the farmlands located in the east of Germany. Now, the Americans and the British found themselves having to provide food, at their own expense, to feed the populations of their own zones.

Clay was convinced that the zonal barriers in Germany had to be broken down. He argued that this was the only way of ensuring that Germany would be able to stand on its own feet economically. In July 1946, with the approval of the American government, Clay offered to unite the American zone with the zone of any other occupying power which was willing to cooperate. Clay had a political objective as well as an economic one. He told James Byrnes, Marshall's predecessor as Secretary of State:

If agreement cannot be obtained along these broad lines in the immediate future, we face a deteriorating German economy which will create political unrest favourable to the development of communism in Germany. (Yergin, *Shattered Peace*)

Already, therefore, at the back of Clay's mind, the idea was developing that in order to save Germany from communism, it might be necessary to break with the Russians and create a separate West Germany out of the Western zones.

The first step in this direction was taken in January 1947. The British and American zones were united to form a single unit – Bizonia. An Economic Council, upon which West German politicians were allowed to sit,

23 General Lucius D. Clay, the American military governor in Germany at the time of the Berlin blockade.

of agreements which included a joint economic policy for the Western zones and the preparation of a constitution for a separate West German state. At the same time, the Western powers announced that they intended to introduce a new currency in the Western zones of Germany and the Western sectors of Berlin. The new currency would replace the old German marks, which had become practically worthless.

The Russians watched these developments with mounting concern. They argued that the Western powers had broken the agreement reached at Potsdam that Germany should be treated as a single economic unit. They decided to introduce a new currency of their own, which was intended to apply throughout the whole of Berlin, West as well as East. They also responded with the Berlin blockade. On 24 June 1948 they announced that owing to 'technical' difficulties, rail traffic between the Western zones of Germany and the Western sectors of Berlin had been suspended. By 4 August, road and canal transport had also been stopped.

Even before the Western powers announced their decision to introduce a new currency, Clay realized that the Russians would be forced to act. Currency was clearly not the major issue at stake. The Russians wanted to put pressure on the Western powers to abandon their plans to create a separate West German state. Clay also realized that Berlin was the most vulnerable spot for the Western powers in the whole of Germany. He believed that the consequences would be enormous if the Western powers gave in by pulling out of West Berlin. He wrote on the eve of the confrontation:

You will understand, of course, that our separate currency reform in the near future followed by a partial German government in Frankfurt will develop the real crisis . . . . Why are we in Europe? We have lost Czechoslovakia. We have lost Finland. Norway is threatened. We retreat from Berlin . . . . After Berlin will come West Germany . . . . If we mean that we are to hold Europe against communism, we must not budge . . . . If America does not believe the issue is cast

was set up to assist in the administration of the enlarged zone. A further step was taken in July 1947 when the three Western zones of Germany became part of the Committee on European Economic Cooperation, which had been established to administer the Marshall Plan. The French lagged behind the Americans and British. They were worried that the Germans might become powerful again. But eventually, the French fell into line.

In February-March 1948, the French joined the Americans and British and representatives from the Benelux countries (Belgium, the Netherlands and Luxembourg) at a conference in London. The Russians were not invited. In June 1948, the conference ended with a series now, then it never will and communism will run rampant. I believe the future of democracy requires us to stay here until forced out. God knows this is not a heroic pose because there will be nothing heroic in having to take humiliation without retaliation. (Mark Arnold-Foster, *The Siege of Berlin*)

Given what was at stake, Clay argued that drastic measures were required. He suggested an armoured breakthrough by road to break the blockade:

I am . . . convinced that a determined movement of convoys with troop protection would reach Berlin and that this might well prevent, rather than build up, Soviet pressures which could lead to war. Nevertheless, I realise fully the dangers inherent in this proposal, since once committed we could not withdraw. (Foster, *Siege*)

But the American government was not prepared to take such a risk. Unsure of how Stalin might react, Truman and his advisers feared that war might result. Instead, the Western powers decided to mount an airlift to West Berlin.

At the beginning, the Western powers did not see the airlift as a solution. They did not believe that it would be possible to fly in sufficient supplies.

When he wrote his own account of the crisis, Clay recalled the difficulties:

Our food stocks on hand were sufficient to last for 36 days and our coal stocks for 45. These stocks had been built up with considerable difficulty as our transportation into Berlin was never adequate . . . . We could sustain a minimum economy with an average daily airlift of 4000 tons and 500 tons for the allied occupation forces. The minimum would not maintain industrial output or provide for domestic heating and normal consumer requirements, and even if coal could be brought into Berlin in unlimited quantities, the electrical generating capacity in the Western sectors was limited because the Russians had removed the equipment of most of its modern plant before we entered the city. Electricity from the Soviet zone was cut off when

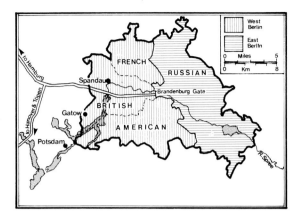

24 Map of Berlin, showing the four sections of occupation. The map also locates Spandau where Rudolph Hess was held in prison until his death in 1987.

the blockade was imposed. The capacity which remained could provide electricity for essential purposes only a few hours each day, and even these hours of use had to be staggered for the various parts of Western Berlin. Despite these conditions we had confidence that its people were prepared to face severe physical suffering rather than live under totalitarian government, that they would endure much hardship to retain their freedom. The resources which we had within the theatre to defeat the blockade were limited. Our transport and troop-carrier planes, more than 100 in number, were C.47s, twin-engined planes of about 2½ tons cargo capacity, and many of them had seen hard war service. The British resources were even more limited. There were no French transport planes available. (Lucius D. Clay, *Decision in Germany*)

At first, therefore, the airlift was mounted to give the Western powers time in which to negotiate. It was also designed to keep up the morale of the West Berliners. But in the event, the Western powers far exceeded their own expectations of what could be achieved. More and bigger planes were made available. By the end of 1948, a plane was taking off for West Berlin from the Western zones of Germany every ninety seconds. A daily average of 7000 tons of supplies was flown in. On a record day in April 1949, one month before the Russians lifted the blockade, 1398 separate flights flew in 13,000 tons of supplies.

The airlift was a considerable technical achievement. It demonstrated beyond all doubt the significance of air power in the modern world. But it was not without its tragedies. Seventy-six people, mainly American and British pilots, were killed. The people of West Berlin showed enormous courage and determination during the blockade. They suffered the hardships without complaint. They were also extremely grateful to those who had helped them. They set up a fund to look after the dependants of the pilots who lost their lives.

West Berlin was saved but it remained an island in a hostile sea. Not until 1971 did the United States, the Soviet Union, Britain and France reach an agreement which eased the travel restrictions between West Berlin and West Germany. The Berlin blockade of 1948-49 was decisive in shaping the future of post-war Europe. The North Atlantic Treaty and the division of Germany followed hard on its heels. It was also a major tactical blunder by the Russians. As Clay put it when it was all over, the blockade was 'the stupidest move the Russians could make'.

25 Unloading a plane at Gatow airport, West Berlin, in July 1948 during the blockade. The target time for unloading a plane was four minutes.

Konrad Adenauer (1876-1967)

Konrad Adenauer was nearly 70 when the war ended in 1945. He had been mayor of Cologne before the Nazis came to power in Germany in 1933. Fearing reprisals against his family, Adenauer never joined the German resistance movement against Hitler. But he was always a suspect in the eyes of the Gestapo. He was arrested in 1944 and spent two months in a concentration camp. At the end of the war he was reinstated as mayor of Cologne but he had several disagreements with the British military authorities. He was dismissed by the British and banned from political activity. The ban was later lifted and he became chairman of the Christian Democratic Union, a new conservative political party. When the Federal Republic of West Germany was established in 1949, Adenauer formed a coalition government and became the first chancellor. He held this position for the next 14 years.

Adenauer was a major influence in shaping the future of post-war Europe. At the end of the war, he was convinced that Europe and therefore Germany would be divided. He wrote in October 1945:

Russia holds the Eastern half of Germany, Poland, the Balkans, apparently Hungary, and a part of Austria. Russia is withdrawing more and more from co-operation with the other great powers and directs affairs in the countries dominated by her entirely as she sees fit. The countries ruled by her are already governed by economic and political principles that are totally different from those accepted in the rest of Europe. Thus the division of Europe into Eastern Europe, the Russian territory, and Western Europe is a fact. (Konrad Adenauer, *Memoirs 1945-53*)

Under these circumstances, Adenauer believed that Western Europe, including those parts of Germany not under Russian control, should join together in a United States of Western Europe. He saw this as a long-term objective. It would be achieved in stages, first through economic and then through political co-operation.

According to Adenauer, a United Western Europe was necessary for two reasons. First, it would make Western Europe strong against the Soviet Union in Eastern Europe. Secondly, it would make Germany's western neighbours, particularly France, feel more secure. Rivalry between France and Germany had been a major cause of the two wars which had been fought in Europe in the twentieth century. Franco-German co-operation was, according to Adenauer, the only way of ending this rivalry. Friendship with France was therefore one of Adenauer's key objectives.

Fortunately for Adenauer, many French politicians shared his vision of a United Western Europe. Although France wanted safeguards against Germany (a fact which explains why France did not hand back to West Germany the industrial region of the Saar until 1957), French politicians agreed with General de Gaulle when he declared in August 1945: 'Frenchmen and Germans must let bygones be bygones, must work together, and must remember that they are Europeans.' A significant step forward in Franco-German co-operation was taken in 1950 when Robert Schuman, the French foreign minister, proposed that France and West Germany should share their coal and steel resources. Schuman's proposal led to the establishment of the European Coal and Steel Community (ECSC) in 1952, when France and West Germany, together with Italy and the Benelux countries, reached agreement on the joint production of coal and steel. The ECSC was the forerunner of the EEC – the European Economic Community or Common Market – which was established in 1957.

Adenauer also believed that full co-operation between West Germany and her western neighbours would not be possible unless West Germany was treated as an equal. But in this respect he did not at first have a free hand. When the state of West Germany was created in 1949, Adenauer's government was not fully independent. The occupying powers – the United States, Britain and France – continued to exercise a number of controls over West Germany's industrial production and over West Germany's foreign policy. Adenauer pressed for the ending of these controls. The issue of West German rearmament presented him with his opportunity.

The idea of allowing West Germany to re-arm was extremely controversial. It arose because of the outbreak of the Korean War in the Far East in 1950. When communist North Korea attacked the non-communist South, the Western powers believed that the communist powers were planning a campaign

26 Konrad Adenauer (second right), the first Chancellor of West Germany, with military commanders of the Western sectors of Germany, April 1950.

27 Franco-West German reconciliation. Adenauer (*right*) with Georges Bidault, the French foreign minister, in March 1954.

of communist expansion. Western Europe was said to be in danger. The Americans insisted that West Germany should be allowed to rearm so that Western Europe would be able to defend itself. In 1950, France proposed a European Defence Community (EDC). Under this proposal, the six countries which eventually formed the ECSC would establish a West European army under joint military command. Once the EDC had come into force, the remaining allied controls in West Germany would be lifted.

Ironically, however, the French National Assembly (parliament) rejected the EDC in 1954. France had not foreseen in 1950 that over the next four years the bulk of the French army would be tied up fighting a colonial war in Indo-China. French politicians now feared that the EDC would be dominated by troops from West Germany. Adenauer was furious. With the French rejection of the EDC, the allied controls in West Germany remained in force. Fortunately, the situation was saved by another suggestion that West Germany should be allowed to contribute to NATO. Upon this

basis, the allied controls were ended in 1954 and West Germany became part of NATO in 1955.

The idea of West German rearmament was particularly controversial within West Germany itself. After their experience under the Nazis, the West German people were not enthusiastic. Adenauer recalled in his memoirs,

A German defence contribution was certainly unpopular in the Federal Republic. I was very disturbed by the attitude of the people. The Germans had got into a state of mind as a result of the war and the post-war period in which they valued freedom, but did not seem prepared to make any sacrifice for it.

Rearmament was opposed on moral grounds by many church leaders. It was also strongly condemned by the Social Democrats, the main opposition party. The Social Democrats argued that West German rearmament and membership of NATO would make it impossible for Germany to be reunited. Stalin, who feared West German rearmament, attempted to stop it in 1952 by proposing a reunified but neutral Germany. But Western governments, and Adenauer in particular, rejected the Russian offer. Adenauer believed that the Russians wanted control over the whole of Germany, and, ultimately, the whole world:

I had become more and more firmly convinced that Stalin had always intended to get hold of West Germany with as little destruction as possible. His policy of the first post-war years had not brought the result he wished, but I was convinced that the Soviet Union had not given it up. If Stalin were to succeed in gaining control in the Federal Republic without too much destruction, he would then be able to exercise a decisive influence on France and Italy, countries whose political order was not very firm and where there were strong communist parties. Soviet dominance in the Federal Republic, France and Italy would make Soviet Russia into the strongest economic, military, and political power on earth. It would mean the victory of communism in the world, including the United States. My policy has always been informed by the conviction that this is the goal of Soviet Russia. (Adenauer, *Memoirs*)

Adenauer had equally firm views on the question of German reunification:

The most important task facing the Federal Government . . . was to do everything to undo the division of our fatherland. In the Soviet zone the German population had no free will of its own. What was done there did not have the support of a free population and thus had no legitimacy. The Federal Republic, on the other hand, was based on the freely expressed will of about 23 million Germans who were entitled to vote. The Federal Republic was therefore the only legitimate political organization of the German people until German unity was achieved . . . . The Federal Republic also felt and still feels a responsibility for the fate of the 19 million Germans who live in the Soviet zone. The Federal Republic alone was and is entitled to

speak for the German people. (Adenauer, *Memoirs*)

Adenauer refused to recognize the government of East Germany. He believed that West Germany needed NATO support to achieve German reunification. To gain that support, West Germany had to fulfil its obligations as an alliance member. His policy made it less likely that Germany would be reunited but at the time there seemed no alternative. His view of the Soviet Union was fully supported by other Western governments.

Adenauer resigned as Chancellor of West Germany in 1963 at the age of 87. Since then his successors have shown greater flexibility in their attitude towards East Germany. Relations have improved in terms both of trade and of human contacts. But to this day, West Germany does not accept that the division of Germany is permanent. There might be two German states but according to the government of West Germany there is still only one German nation.

Walter Ulbricht (1893-1973)

Born in Leipzig, the son of a tailor, Walter Ulbricht was apprenticed as a carpenter. He learned his early socialism from his parents and joined the German Socialist Youth Movement at the age of 13. In 1910 he became a member of the German Socialist Party and in 1919 he was one of the co-founders of the German Communist Party. He spent the next few years in Moscow learning about the organization of the Soviet Communist Party. When he returned to Germany, he was elected as a communist deputy or MP in the Reichstag, the German parliament. But when Hitler came to power in 1933 the communists were outlawed. Ulbricht had to leave Germany and took refuge in the Soviet Union. He fought on the Republican side during the Spanish Civil War and spent the Second

World War in the Soviet Union. He was flown back to Berlin by the Russians in April 1945.

According to his biographer, Carola Stern, Ulbricht was not a particularly attractive personality:

Even as a young Leipzig Communist, Walter Ulbricht was not very charming. He could not win friends – either for himself or for his cause. He lacked social graces, charm, persuasiveness, rhetorical gifts, originality, brilliance, education, imagination, and the vitality of the passionate revolutionary. He lacked style. He would not become a truly popular spokesman for he was unable to inspire the masses. He was simply not the type of man who came, saw, and conquered. So he had to work his way up through the machine and learn the trade of Party hack. His talents in this realm made him a useful Communist organizer. (Carola Stern, *Walter Ulbricht: A Political Biography*)

Ulbricht excelled in the detailed problems of day-to-day administration. In 1925 he wrote an article about party organization in a neighbourhood cell, the equivalent of a ward in a British local election:

House-to-house agitation and propaganda play an important part in the neighbourhood cell. Each comrade should be assigned certain houses. Discussions with workers and their wives can be tied in with door-to-door selling of newspaper subscriptions and Party literature. Comrades whose jobs take them into the homes of workers, employees, and civil servants can easily carry on agitation. Casual encounters in stores and markets, at the barber, in restaurants and hallways, can also be used for propaganda purposes. It is important to talk to servants, janitors, etc., not only to enlighten them but also to get information about their employers. (Stern, *Ulbricht*)

It was as an organizer that Ulbricht rose to the top as one of the leaders of the German communists. He was a typical *apparatchik* – a bureaucrat responsible for the smooth running of the organization of the party. Carola Stern explains how the mind of an *apparatchik* works:

28 Walter Ulbricht (*left*) at the opening of the People's Congress in Berlin, December 1947. Ulbricht led the Socialist Unity Party (the East German Communist party) until his retirement in 1971. On the right is Otto Grotewohl, who became prime minister of East Germany in 1949.

The *apparatchik* obeys the laws of the Party machine. The *apparat* [the party machine] is no place for visionaries; neither is it a place where programmes of 'general policies' are worked out. It is designed for detail work, for plodding. The *apparatchik* does not really care which of the warring factions is victorious – let others worry about these things – just as long as there is a winning political line that he can administer in an orderly manner. Not to know where to turn for authority is his greatest fear. He abhors [detests] factional struggles, with their continual change in leadership and their power crises. All he can do then is to hold the *apparat* together. But give him a strong, entrenched leadership, and he can administer firmly and efficiently.

It is not surprising, therefore, that Ulbricht was a loyal and dedicated Stalinist.

In June 1945, two months after Ulbricht arrived back in Berlin, the Russian military government issued an order permitting the formation of political parties in the Eastern zone of Germany. Four parties came into being: the Christian Democrats or Conservatives, the Social Democrats, the Communists and the Free Democrats or Liberals. The socialists wanted to merge with the communists to form a united left-wing party. Ulbricht hesitated because the communists were not ready. But he changed his mind at the end of 1945. He realised that the communists were losing out to the socialists in the race to win the political support of the working class. Resenting the manner in which the Russians dismantled their factories and transported them to the Soviet Union, the workers were more inclined to support the socialists. The communists were handicapped because they were so closely associated with the Russian military government.

In order to regain support, the communists agreed to merge with the socialists. The merger took place in April 1946, when a new party – the Socialist Unity Party (SED) – was created. The party had its own programme based on the 'German way to Socialism'. It also had joint leaders. Otto Grotewohl, a socialist, and Wilhelm Pieck, a communist, were appointed joint chairmen. Ulbricht became general secretary in control of the party organization. The Western powers refused to allow the SED to operate in the Western zones of Germany.

The nature of the SED changed from the autumn of 1947. As relations between East and West deteriorated, the party was purged of 'enemies within the ranks'. The purges grew more intense in 1948, as a result of the quarrel between Stalin and Tito's Yugoslavia. Stalin was determined to ensure that communist parties elsewhere in Eastern Europe did not follow Tito's example. Membership of the SED dropped from 2 million to 1.8 million. The idea of building a German way to Socialism was abandoned. The SED had to follow the Soviet example, which emphasized the development of heavy industry. At the same time it had to adopt the organization of the Soviet Communist Party. The SED became a communist party in all but name.

When the German Democratic Republic was established in October 1949, Otto Grotewohl became prime minister. But real power rested with Ulbricht as general secretary of the SED. The early years were difficult ones for East Germany. In order to build a socialist economy as rapidly as possible, Ulbricht was only too ready to copy Soviet methods. He made the development of heavy industry his priority. He refused to invest in light industry to make more consumer goods available. The East German population grew restless. Living standards in

neighbouring West Germany were much higher. In June 1953 popular unrest spilled over. Riots and demonstrations on the streets of East Berlin forced Ulbricht to leave the capital. He took refuge on a farm outside the city, near a Soviet airfield. He did not return until Russian tanks had appeared in East Berlin to put down the disturbances.

Ulbricht had to accept responsibility for the events of 1953. He humbled himself by confessing to the Central Committee of the SED:

I would like to say openly before the highest forum of the Party that among Party leaders I bear the greatest responsibility . . . for the errors that have been committed. (Stern, *Ulbricht*)

Economically, Ulbricht changed course. The production of consumer goods was expanded with Russian financial help. But still the economy did not improve. Next door, West Germany was prospering and proving an irresistible attraction for many East Germans. They voted with their feet and crossed the border which divided Berlin in search of jobs and a new way of life in the West. By 1960, East Germany had lost about two million of its original population of 19 million. The majority who left were young and skilled, the very people East Germany could least afford to lose. To stop people leaving, the East Germans put up the Berlin Wall in August 1961. Border guards were ordered to shoot to kill if people tried to escape. But the Berlin Wall had one positive effect. By stopping the flood of people leaving, it enabled the East Germans to plan their economy and to improve living standards.

Ulbricht was one of the longest serving survivors of the Stalin era in Eastern Europe. Abroad, he was mainly concerned to gain international recognition of East Germany as an independent state. The question of recognition was a major stumbling block in the improvement of relations between East and West Germany. Ulbricht resigned in 1971. As in the case of Adenauer, Ulbricht's departure opened the way for closer ties between the two German states.

29 East German border guards supervise the construction of the Berlin Wall, September 1961.

THE ATOM BOMB: SCIENTISTS AND SPIES

On 6 and 9 August 1945 two atomic bombs were dropped on the Japanese cities of Hiroshima and Nagasaki. The exact number of those killed in the two blasts, either at the time or over a period of time, will probably never be known. Estimates of the number killed at the time at Hiroshima vary from 78,000 to 200,000. The figure for Nagasaki is estimated at 100,000. But if the death toll was uncertain, one thing was perfectly clear. The age of nuclear weapons had begun.

A number of revisionists have argued that the bombs were dropped not to defeat Japan but to warn the Russians. But this is a minority view. Most historians agree that the bombs were dropped in order to end the war quickly and to avoid the heavy casualties which would have resulted had the Americans been forced to invade Japan.

At Potsdam, Truman told Stalin that the United States had a new weapon of 'unusual destructive force'. Stalin was not unduly concerned. He simply said that he was glad to hear the news and that he hoped the Americans would make good use of the weapon against Japan. Truman was puzzled by Stalin's reaction. He did not realize that Stalin knew all about the atomic bomb. For a number of years Western spies had been passing on technical secrets about the bomb to Soviet agents.

Only a handful of Westerners had been spying for the Russians. But they included diplomats, military personnel and scientists. These were people who worked in sensitive areas of government. The details of their activities became known in 1949-50. This was the worst possible time for the American government. Helped by the information which had been passed on to them, the Russians had tested an atomic bomb of their own in July 1949.

The American government was astonished because it believed that the Russians were a long way behind in the development of atomic weapons. In October 1949, a civil war in China ended in victory for the communists. The American government was embarrassed. American money and equipment had been used in an attempt to prop up the Nationalist government of China. Right-wing critics of Truman's government began to search for scapegoats to explain these setbacks. They found them in the State Department. In February 1950, Joseph McCarthy, the junior Republican Senator from Wisconsin, made the startling allegation that he had the names of 205 people employed in the State Department who were communist sympathizers. America was about to be swept by a wave of 'McCarthyism'. By means of smear campaigns and half-truths, well known American liberals and intellectuals were accused of belonging to communist-front organizations. The House of

30 The Japanese city of Hiroshima after the first atomic bomb was dropped in August 1945.

31 Senator Joseph McCarthy, who led the witch-hunt for communists and subversives in America in the early 1950s.

Representatives revived its pre-war Committee on Un-American Activities. All manner of people – from scientists to movie stars – were paraded before the Committee. They faced ruthless questioning about their friendships and their political beliefs. Government employees and potential employees had to submit themselves to a loyalty test. Between 1947 and 1952, over 4½ million people were screened but only 560 were either dismissed or refused employment. For the most part, McCarthy's accusations were based on a gigantic lie but the 'red scare' which he created helped win the 1952 election for the Republicans. Aided by prominent Republicans, such as the future president, Richard Nixon, McCarthy continued his campaign for the next two years. He was finally undone in 1954 when he rashly began making accusations against President Eisenhower, Truman's successor.

This chapter is based on the careers of two scientists who played major roles in the story of the atom bomb. First, Robert Oppenheimer, director of the Manhattan Project who became known as the 'Father of the Atom Bomb'. Secondly, Klaus Fuchs, a German scientist granted British citizenship who became a spy and passed on atomic secrets to the Russians.

Robert Julius Oppenheimer (1904-1967)

Robert Oppenheimer was born in New York and came from a family of wealthy German-Jewish immigrants. He was educated at Harvard, Cambridge and Göttingen University in Sweden, from where he gained his PhD in 1927. On his return to the United States he became a lecturer at the Berkeley and Pasadena campuses of the University of California. Throughout the 1930s he built up a reputation as a theoretical physicist and made several important contributions to atomic theory.

Oppenheimer also became interested in left-wing politics in the 1930s. Important influences were his brother Frank and Jean Tatlock, Oppenheimer's girlfriend before his marriage to Kathryn Puening in 1940. Frank and Jean Tatlock were both members of the American Communist Party. In later life Oppenheimer denied having been a member of the Communist Party himself but he was certainly active in a number of left-wing organizations which had close links with the communists. Prominent amongst these was the Teachers' Union, a radical body which supported the cause of social reform at home and resistance to fascism abroad. Oppenheimer was attracted to communism in the 1930s because of the depression in the United States and because the liberal democracies in Western Europe (Britain and France) had done so little to combat fascism. He supported the republican left during the Spanish Civil War and donated money to Spanish war relief groups. He also made donations to funds associated with the American Communist Party and wrote a number of articles defending the policies of the Soviet Union. Oppenheimer made no secret about his left-wing past. Looking back, he told *Time* magazine in 1948:

I became a real left-winger, joined the teachers' union, had lots of Communist friends. It was what most people do in college or late high school . . . I'm not ashamed of it. I'm more ashamed of the lateness. Most of what I believed then now seems complete nonsense, but it was an essential part of becoming a whole man. If it hadn't been for this late but indispensable education, I couldn't have done the job at Los Alamos at all. (Goodchild, *Oppenheimer*)

In 1942, Oppenheimer was chosen as director of the Manhattan project to develop an American atomic bomb. He helped to select the site for the laboratory at Los Alamos in New Mexico. As director, he had to deal with a team of several hundred scientists and scores of politicians and generals who were interested in the project. He was also kept under close surveillance by the American security and intelligence services who were assigned to the Manhattan project.

Because of his left-wing past, Oppenheimer

32 Robert Oppenheimer (in hat) with fellow scientists from the Manhattan Project.

was not given security clearance until 1943. A number of security officers became obsessed with the idea that he was a security risk and that he might pass on secrets to his communist friends. His mail was opened, his telephone was tapped, his office was bugged and his every movement was watched and noted. Despite the elaborate security checks, no hard evidence was found against him.

At the beginning of 1943 an incident occurred which turned out to be one of the most important in Oppenheimer's life. Enjoying a break from the Los Alamos laboratory at his home in Berkeley, Oppenheimer invited an old friend, Haakon Chevalier, and his wife round for dinner. Chevalier was a communist and one-time president of the Teachers' Union. Over dinner when the two men were alone, Chevalier mentioned that George Eltenton, a British engineer working for Shell in California, had means of getting technical information to the Russians. Whether Chevalier was trying to persuade Oppenheimer to pass on information, or whether he simply felt that Oppenheimer should be aware of Eltenton's existence, remains uncertain.

Oppenheimer made it clear that he would have no part in any such dealings but he did not immediately report the incident. Later in 1943, Oppenheimer was questioned by security officers about the overall level of security at Los Alamos. Of his own accord, he mentioned the name of Eltenton. He also revealed that another contact had made approaches to three other scientists working at Los Alamos. Oppenheimer said that the approaches had been made because a number of people believed that there was insufficient technical co-operation with the Russians, America's ally in the war. Espionage, he said, was not the motive. At first, Oppenheimer refused to reveal the identity of the other contact. Questioned further, he was then ordered to reveal the name. Reluctantly, Oppenheimer gave the name of Chevalier. He did not, however, reveal that he was one of the three scientists whom Chevalier had approached. A close watch was still kept on Oppenheimer but, for the time being, the Chevalier incident was dropped.

In April 1945, a month before Germany surrendered in Europe, Oppenheimer was able to report that an atomic bomb would be ready by August. America's military chiefs were keen to use the bomb because it would make the planned invasion of Japan unnecessary, shorten the war and save the lives of thousands of American soldiers. But some of the scientists working at Los Alamos were uncertain. Their doubts were based on moral grounds and they wondered whether it might be possible to arrange a demonstration of the bomb which would frighten the Japanese and force them to surrender. The government appointed a committee of scientists, politicians and generals to consider the question. Oppenheimer, who was one of the scientists on the committee, did not share the doubts of his colleagues. He argued that a demonstration might not work and that the Japanese might move American prisoners into the demonstration area. He therefore supported the committee's three recommendations: first, that the bomb should be used against Japan; secondly, that the target should be a military one surrounded by a civilian population; and finally, that no prior warning should be given.

Oppenheimer was present when the atomic bomb was tested just before dawn at Alamogordo in the desert of New Mexico on 16 July 1945. 'A few people laughed, a few people cried, most people were silent', was how Oppenheimer recalled the reaction of the watching scientists. He used a line from one of ancient India's epic tales to describe his own reaction:

There floated through my mind a line from the *Bhagavadgita* in which Krishna is trying to persuade the Prince that he should do his duty: 'I am become death, the shatterer of worlds.' (Goodchild, *Oppenheimer*)

Three weeks later, on 6 August, the first atomic bomb was dropped on Hiroshima. When news of the drop reached Los Alamos, Oppenheimer was jubilant. He called a meeting of the entire staff of the laboratory. A scientist described the scene:

He [Oppenheimer] entered that meeting like a prize fighter. As he walked through the hall there were cheers and shouts and applause all round and he acknowledged them with the fighters' salute – clasping his hands together above his head as he came to the podium. (Goodchild, *Oppenheimer*)

But the sense of triumph was shortlived. On 21 August, just two weeks after the second drop on Nagasaki, Harry Daghlian, a young scientist, received a lethal dose of radiation when one of the small bricks of uranium he was assembling at the Los Alamos laboratory slipped. He developed second-degree burns on his hands and chest and a fever developed. After two weeks the burns blistered and he lost his hair. He died a month later.

Even before the Daghlian accident, Oppenheimer's attitude had changed. He told the army of reporters milling around the laboratory that he was 'a little scared of what I have made'. Although he also told the reporters that a scientist 'cannot hold back progress because of fears of what the world will do with his discoveries', he was now anxious to get away from Los Alamos. He left the laboratory on 16 October 1945. In his parting speech he declared:

If atomic bombs are to be added to the arsenals of a warring world, or to the arsenals of nations preparing for war, the time will come when mankind will curse the name of Los Alamos and Hiroshima. (Goodchild, *Oppenheimer*)

Oppenheimer returned to his teaching career at the Pasadena campus of the University of California. He used his influence to press for international control of atomic energy. In 1946, the United Nations established an Atomic Energy Commission. The Commission failed to produce a formula for international control, largely because of differences between the United States and the Soviet Union. The American government decided to set up its own Atomic Energy Commission. It also appointed a General Advisory Committee to advise the Commission on scientific and technical matters. Oppenheimer was the natural choice to become the Committee's chairman.

33 The laboratory buildings at Los Alamos, New Mexico, where the first atomic bomb was produced.

One of the key questions before the Committee was whether or not the United States should give priority to the development of a more powerful hydrogen bomb. Oppenheimer had firm views on this question:

What concerns me is really not the technical problem. I am not sure the miserable thing will work, nor that it can be gotten to a target except by ox cart . . . . What does worry me is that this thing appears to have caught the imagination of the Congressional and of military people, as the answer to the problem posed by the Russian advance. It would be folly to oppose the exploration of this weapon. We have always known it had to be done, and it does have to be done . . . . But that we become committed to it as the way to save the country and the peace appears to me full of dangers. (Goodchild, *Oppenheimer*)

Oppenheimer's colleagues on the Advisory Committee shared these views. In October 1949 the Committee concluded:

We all hope that by one means or another, the development of these weapons can be avoided. We are all reluctant to see the United States take the initiative in precipitating this development. We are all agreed that it would be wrong at present to commit ourselves to an all-out effort towards its development. (Goodchild, *Oppenheimer*)

The timing of the Committee's conclusion could not have been more unfortunate. The Soviet Union had just alarmed the United States by testing an atomic bomb. Then, in January 1950, Klaus Fuchs was arrested in Britain. Fuchs admitted that he had passed on information to the Russians while working on the Los Alamos project. The United States was swept by a wave of anti-communist hysteria and Senator Joseph McCarthy began making his allegations about communist sympathizers in government departments. Shaken by these developments, President Truman announced that the United States intended to press ahead with the development of the hydrogen bomb.

The next few years were increasingly difficult for Oppenheimer. He became the subject of a number of security investigations by the Federal Bureau of Investigation (FBI). The net tightened around him when President Eisenhower took office in January 1953. A new security order was issued. All government employees were now required to have a background which was 'clearly consistent with the interests of national security'. The FBI moved in for the kill. They presented a dossier on Oppenheimer and argued that his security clearance should be withdrawn. The FBI case was largely based on Oppenheimer's pre-war activities and his opposition to the hydrogen bomb. The case was presented to Eisenhower, who decided that there should be a full investigation. The Atomic Energy Commission appointed a three-man Security Board to sit in judgement. Effectively, Oppenheimer was put on trial for treason.

The case against Oppenheimer was heard for four weeks in April-May 1954. A number of witnesses were called, including Oppenheimer himself. He was questioned about his left-wing past, his association with Jean Tatlock and, of course, the Chevalier incident. He was forced to admit that he had lied about being approached by Chevalier. The verdict of the Security Board was announced in May. By a two to one majority, the Board recommended that Oppenheimer's security clearance should be withdrawn.

The findings of the two Board members who decided against Oppenheimer made extraordinary reading. They described Oppenheimer as a 'loyal citizen'. They also judged that Oppenheimer 'seems to have had a high degree of discretion, reflecting an unusual ability to keep to himself vital secrets'. But on the crucial question of the hydrogen bomb, their statement declared:

We cannot dismiss the matter of Dr Oppenheimer's relationship to the development of the hydrogen bomb, simply with the finding that his conduct was not motivated by disloyalty, because it is our conclusion that, whatever the motivation, the security interests of the United States were affected.

We believe that, had Dr Oppenheimer given his enthusiastic support to the program, a concerted effort would have been initiated at an earlier date. (Goodchild, *Oppenheimer*)

In other words, the two Board members decided against Oppenheimer, not because he was disloyal, still less because he was a practical security risk, but because he had been so effective in making known his views about the hydrogen bomb. Sam Goudsmit, an old colleague of Oppenheimer's, commented at the time:

I do not imply that Oppenheimer's advice is always right and should be heeded, but if advisers, whose strong convictions are occasionally not shared by the administration are called disloyal, differences of opinion, which form the basis of democratic rule, would soon be replaced by totalitarian conformity. (Goodchild, *Oppenheimer*)

Small wonder then that Peter Goodchild, author of a biography of Oppenheimer, should describe the Oppenheimer case as a 'travesty of justice'.

Oppenheimer's security clearance was never reinstated. He retired to academic life and became a popular speaker on his lecture tours. Towards the end of his life the American government made a number of gestures which indicated that the verdict against him had been wrong. In 1963 he was given the Fermi Award (named after Enrico Fermi, one of the Los Alamos scientists) by the Atomic Energy Commission. He died of cancer of the throat in 1967.

Klaus Fuchs (1911-1988)

Dr Klaus Fuchs was a German physicist who joined the German Communist Party in 1930. At Keil University he was beaten up by the Nazi brownshirts because of his beliefs. When Hitler came to power in 1933 he had to leave Germany. He went to France first and then to Britain. He worked as a research scientist at Bristol and Edinburgh Universities.

In 1934 the German consul at Bristol told the local chief constable that Fuchs was a communist. But since he had not joined the British Communist Party and was not involved in communist activities, the report was dismissed as a Nazi attempt to discredit him. However, with Britain at war, Fuchs was interned as an enemy alien in 1940. Together with many other Germans living in Britain, he was sent to a detention camp in Canada. Pressure from his fellow scientists in Britain secured his release in 1941. Back in Britain he signed the Official Secrets Act and worked at Birmingham University on a project to develop an atomic bomb. Fuchs never made any secret of his communist sympathies but the British intelligence authorities ignored this aspect of his past and gave him security clearance. In 1942 he was granted British citizenship.

Taking advantage of his access to top secret information, Fuchs began passing vital technical secrets to Soviet agents. Through a friend in the British Communist Party he contacted Alexander, the codename for the Military Attaché's Secretary at the Soviet Embassy in London. Fuchs had weekend meetings with his contact in the Kensington area of London. He handed over carbon copies of his official reports and handwritten notes. Fuchs was later introduced to a German-Jewish refugee codenamed Sonya, a Russian spy based at Oxford. Meetings took place in country lanes near Banbury. In

34 Klaus Fuchs, whose espionage enabled the Russians to test an atomic bomb much sooner than Western scientists had anticipated.

November 1943, Fuchs was sent to the United States to join the American atomic research team working on the Manhattan project at Los Alamos in New Mexico. Sonya had given him instructions to make contact with Raymond, a Soviet agent in the United States. Raymond was the codename for Heinrich Golodnitsky, a Swiss Jew, who had taken the name Harry Gold when his parents emigrated to the United States in 1941. Fuchs had several meetings with Gold and handed over plans for the construction of the atom bomb. The two men met again after the bombs had been dropped on Hiroshima and Nagasaki. Fuchs gave Gold an eye-witness account of the test explosion in New Mexico and also passed on all he knew about the two bombs dropped on Japan – their size, the materials used and how the bombs were detonated.

Fuchs returned to Britain in June 1946. He worked at the research institute of the British Atomic Energy Commission, which was based at Harwell in Berkshire. Within a year, he was again passing on secrets to the Russians. Over the next two years he had about eight meetings with Soviet agents. The meetings took place in two London pubs – the Spotted Horse in Putney High Street and the Nag's Head in Wood Green. Eventually, it became clear to both American and British intelligence that secrets were being passed on to the Russians. Fuchs became a prime suspect. He was uncovered in 1949 when American cipher experts managed to break Soviet intelligence codes. In Britain, Fuchs was questioned by James Skardon, a senior MI5 officer. At first Fuchs denied his Russian contacts but then he made a full confession. He startled Skardon by saying, almost casually, that the worst thing he had done was to tell the Russians how to make an atomic bomb. Arrested in January 1950, Fuchs was put on trial at the Old Bailey and sentenced to fourteen years imprisonment.

In his confession, the major piece of evidence at his trial, Fuchs revealed that he separated his mind into what he described as two compartments. His loyalty to communism and to the Soviet Union represented the first compartment. He believed, as did many other left-wing intellectuals of the 1930s and 1940s, that communism alone was capable of building a society based on justice and equality.

Fuchs' second compartment represented his personal life, and, in particular, his personal friendships with his fellow scientists. He described in his confession how he managed to separate this second compartment from the first:

In the course of this work I began naturally to form bonds of personal friendship and I had to conceal from them my inner thoughts. I used my Marxist philosophy to establish in my mind two separate compartments in which I allowed myself to make friendships, to have personal relations, to help people and to be in all personal ways the kind of man I wanted to be, and the kind of man which, in a personal way, I had been before with my friends in or near the Communist Party. I could be free and easy and happy with other people without fear of disclosing myself . . . I could forget the other compartment and still rely on it. It appeared to me at the time that I had become a 'free man' because I had succeeded in the other compartment in establishing myself completely independent of the surrounding forces of society. Looking back on it now the best way of expressing it seems to be to call it a controlled schizophrenia. (H. Montgomery Hyde, *The Atom Bomb Spies*)

The judge at the Old Bailey trial was not impressed by the argument of defence counsel that Fuchs had made his confession voluntarily. Summing up and passing sentence, the judge declared:

In 1933, fleeing from political persecution in Germany, you took advantage of the right of asylum, or the privilege of asylum, which has always been the boast of this country to people persecuted in their own country for their political opinions. You betrayed the hospitality and protection given to you by the greatest treachery . . . . In 1942, in return for your offer to put at the service of this country the great gifts Providence has bestowed on you in scientific matters, you were granted British nationality. From that moment, regardless of your oath, you started to betray secrets of vital importance for the purpose of furthering a political creed [communism] held in abhorrence [hated] by the vast majority in this country, your object being to strengthen that creed which was then known to be inimical [hostile] to all freedom-loving countries. (Hyde, *The Atom Bomb Spies*)

The case of Klaus Fuchs was very embarrassing for Clement Attlee's Labour government. It highlighted a number of defects in the British security services. It also strained relations between the United States and Britain because Fuchs had passed on American secrets while working on the Manhattan project. The Americans responded by banning the flow of atomic secrets to Britain for the next nine years. The evidence presented at the Fuchs trial was used in America to incriminate Julius Rosenberg and his wife Ethel. The Rosenbergs were active communists who passed American military secrets to the Russians. Unlike Fuchs, who was sent to prison, the Rosenbergs were sent to the electric chair.

Fuchs served nine of his fourteen years and was released in 1959. He served the first part of his sentence at Wormwood Scrubs and then at prisons in Stafford and Wakefield. He was a model prisoner who earned full remission. He was generally liked by his fellow prisoners, being generous in sharing his cigarettes and giving them evening classes. When he was released in 1959 he went to East Germany and became deputy director of the Central Institute of Nuclear Research at Rossendorf near Dresden.

TOWARDS THE BRINK: BERLIN AND CUBA

The Cold War in the fifties and early sixties differed significantly from that which had originated in the forties. In the first place, it covered a much wider area. It was no longer confined to Europe. It spread across the world – from the Far East and South-East Asia, to the Near and Middle East, to Central and Latin America, and to Africa.

At the beginning of the 50s, the major conflict areas were the Far East and South-East Asia. The People's Republic – Communist China – was established in October 1949. The 'loss' of China to communism alarmed the United States. The Americans had backed Chiang Kai-shek, the leader of China's nationalist government. When Chiang was overthrown by the communists, the Americans argued that something sinister was happening in China. They believed that the Russians now controlled Mao Zedong's communists.

The Americans were wrong. Mao Zedong was his own man, not Stalin's puppet. But the Americans believed that the Russians were now using the Chinese to expand communism. The Korean War (1950–53) and the French defeat in Indo-China in 1954 reinforced this fear. American and Chinese troops clashed during the Korean War. General Douglas MacArthur, the American commander, wanted to carry the war across the North Korean border into China itself. To restrain MacArthur, President Truman had to sack him. At the beginning of 1953, the new Republican administration of President Eisenhower threatened to use nuclear weapons against China to end the military stalemate. The war eventually ended with an armistice in July 1953.

The extension of the Cold War to other areas of the world brought with it new policies and strategies. Eisenhower's Republicans were not satisfied with the Democrats' policy of containment. John Foster Dulles, Eisenhower's Secretary of State, condemned containment as a weak policy. Dulles believed that containment had allowed the communists to gain control of key areas of the world. Dulles viewed communism as the greatest evil known to mankind. Rather than contain it, he wanted to destroy it. He proclaimed a policy of 'liberation', the idea being to 'roll-back' the frontiers of communist power. Quite how this would be achieved was never explained. Dulles believed that the United States should both defend people against the threat of communism and assist people attempting to free themselves of communist domination. Hungary rebelled against the communist system in 1956. Soviet tanks were sent into Budapest to crush the rebellion. The Americans protested but did nothing. Liberation and roll-back were little more than empty slogans.

35 American troops on the road to the South Korean capital of Seoul during the Korean War, 1950.

America's military strategy in the mid-1950s was equally unrealistic. After Korea, the United States announced that it would not fight any more 'bush-fire' wars. Instead, the Americans declared that they would resort to 'massive retaliation' – the immediate use of nuclear weapons – to deter communist aggression. The problem here was one of credibility. Were the Americans serious about unleashing nuclear weapons, and running the risk of starting a Third World War, for the sake of defending Chiang Kai-shek's nationalists, who were now based in exile on the island of Taiwan? Massive retaliation sent shivers down the spines of America's NATO allies but it was hardly a practical policy.

More concrete changes were taking place in the Soviet Union. When Stalin died in 1953 he was succeeded by a collective leadership from which Nikita Khrushchev emerged as the leading figure. The new Soviet leaders were more flexible than Stalin. They wanted to move away from the Cold War towards a more constructive policy based on the idea of 'peaceful coexistence'. They also wanted to project a more positive image abroad, not only in the West but throughout the Third World as well. Building bridges to the Third World was one of the ways in which the Soviet Union could leapfrog the barriers of containment erected by the United States.

36 Wrecked Soviet tanks in the streets of Budapest during the Hungarian uprising, October 1956. At the time, the Russians condemned the uprising as the work of counter-revolutionaries and reactionaries. Only now are they admitting that it represented a popular revolt.

Unlike Stalin, who seldom travelled abroad, the new Soviet leaders developed a taste for foreign travel. They saw their visits as a test of their own character. They had to overcome their own sense of inferiority when dealing with the West. Khrushchev travelled to Geneva for a summit meeting – the first in ten years – with the leaders of the Western allies in 1955. Discussion at Geneva ranged over a variety of issues. Khrushchev angrily rejected Eisenhower's 'open-skies' proposal, under which each nation would allow aerial surveillance of its military installations. To Khrushchev, open-skies was simply another form of spying. The Geneva summit ended without any practical agreements but Khrushchev was not dissatisfied. The summit had been a test of character. 'All things considered, I would say we passed the test', was Khrushchev's verdict.

Geneva was seen at the time as a breakthrough in East-West relations. More important than the absence of positive results from the summit was the fact that both sides were at least talking to each other again. But the spirit of Geneva did not last long. A huge gulf still separated the two sides. The Berlin problem remained unsolved. The arms race continued. The national liberation struggle in the Third World continued to worry the Americans. The Russians had their own problems, particularly with Communist China. The United States and the Soviet Union were set on a collision course which came to a climax with the two great crises of the early 60s – the Berlin Wall in 1961 and the Cuban missile crisis in 1962.

Important lessons were learned from the Cuban missile crisis. In June 1963 the White House and the Kremlin were linked by a telex known as the 'hot-line'. It enabled the American and Soviet leaders to maintain close contact in any future crisis. In August 1963 the United States and the Soviet Union signed, together with Britain, a Test Ban Treaty which banned the testing of nuclear weapons in the atmosphere, outer space and underwater. But the Test Ban Treaty did not halt the arms race. In fact, the arms race gathered pace as a result of the missile crisis.

Whatever the costs to their domestic economy, the Russians were now determined to match the Americans in terms of inter-continental or strategic missiles. They vowed that they would never again be placed in a position of military inferiority. The Soviet military build-up, together with the Russian invasion of Czechoslovakia in 1968 and America's deep involvement in the Vietnam War, delayed any further high-level Soviet-American negotiations until 1969. In that year a new round of talks began which led to the first SALT (Strategic Arms Limitation Treaty) agreement of 1972. But this is jumping too far ahead, to a different story set in a different time with different people. To demonstrate the nature of the Cold War in the 50s and early 60s, this final chapter examines the careers of three individuals whose names will always be identified with the period when the Cold War very nearly became hot: Nikita Khrushchev, the Soviet leader; Fidel Castro, the Cuban leader; and John F. Kennedy, the American president.

Nikita Sergeyevich Khrushchev (1894-1971)

The name of Nikita Sergeyevich Khrushchev is still one to conjure with. A larger than life character, squat and bald-headed, Khrushchev seemed to dominate international politics in the post-Stalin era. Khrushchev was so unpredictable that people in the West never knew what to make of him. On the one hand, he could be charming, fun-loving and almost comical. On one never-to-be-forgotten occasion, he removed his shoe at a meeting of the United Nations in New York and banged it on the table. But on the other hand, he could be menacing and threatening. Threats and ultimatums were his trademark.

From a mining background, Khrushchev climbed the political ladder in the Soviet Union as one of Stalin's minions. He was the political boss of the Ukraine during the Second World War and in 1949 Stalin made him responsible for the reorganization of Soviet agriculture. In September 1953, six months after Stalin's death, Khrushchev was appointed First Secretary of the Communist Party. He survived an attempt to dismiss him in 1957 and in 1958 he became Prime Minister as well as First Secretary. But it would be wrong to exaggerate Khrushchev's power. To a much greater extent than had been the case with Stalin, Khrushchev was always dependent on the support of the Presidium, the name by which the Politburo was known between 1952 and 1966.

Khrushchev made his most significant mark on the Soviet Union in March 1956 when he addressed the Twentieth Congress of the Soviet Communist Party in Moscow. In his famous 'secret speech' – secret in the sense that it was not made public at the time, the details were leaked to the West later – Khrushchev attacked Stalin. He denounced the personality cult which Stalin had created around himself. He also denounced Stalin's purges against the Communist Party in the 1930s. Khrushchev was careful not to go too far in attacking Stalin. He did not, for instance, mention Stalin's crimes against the Soviet people. To have done this would have been to undermine the entire basis upon which the Communist Party justified its monopoly of political power and its right to rule.

In open session at the Congress, Khrushchev also announced a new departure in Soviet foreign policy. He declared that the Soviet Communist Party recognized the existence of 'different roads to socialism'. By implication, it was no longer necessary for socialist countries to copy the methods of the Soviet Union. Of equal significance, Khrushchev declared that war was no longer inevitable between capitalist and socialist countries. Instead, he argued that it was now possible for countries with different political systems to live together – 'peaceful coexistence' was the term Khrushchev used.

Why did Khrushchev attack Stalin and why did he want to change Soviet foreign policy? The attack on Stalin was designed to rid the Soviet Union of the worst aspects of Stalin's legacy. There would be no more purges and no more personality cults. Khrushchev also wanted to change direction economically. To raise living standards, he wanted to spend more money on agriculture and on the production of consumer goods. As he wrote in his memoirs:

It's time for us to realize that the teachings of Marx, Engels, and Lenin cannot be hammered into people's heads only in the classroom and newspapers and at political rallies; agitation and propaganda on behalf of Soviet power must also be carried on in our restaurants and cafeterias. Our people must be able to use their wages to buy high-quality products manufactured under socialism if they are ultimately to accept our system and reject capitalism. (Strobe Talbot, ed., *Khrushchev Remembers*)

Khrushchev's economic thinking played a major part in his foreign policy. He wanted to reduce the colossal sums of money which the Soviet Union spent on defence. He could only do this by reducing the risk of war. For Khrushchev, war itself was now unthinkable. He had a genuine horror of nuclear war. He therefore argued in favour of peaceful coexistence.

It is important to understand what Khrushchev meant by 'peaceful coexistence'. Like Stalin before him, Khrushchev believed that capitalism was doomed. He had no doubt that socialism would triumph. He wrote in his memoirs:

We Communists, we Marxist-Leninists, believe that progress is on our side and victory will inevitably be ours. Yet the capitalists won't give an inch and still swear to fight to the bitter end. Therefore how can we talk of peaceful coexistence with capitalist ideology? Peaceful coexistence among different systems of government is possible, but peaceful coexistence among different ideologies is not. It would be a betrayal of our Party's first principles to believe that there can be peaceful coexistence between Marxist-Leninist ideology on the one hand and bourgeois ideology on the other. (Talbott, ed., *Khrushchev Remembers*)

How then would the victory of socialism be achieved? For Khrushchev, socialism would triumph not through war but by economic example. He argued that socialism represented a better way of life. He predicted that the Soviet Union would eventually catch up and then overtake the United States in the production of the basics such as food and housing and also luxuries such as motor cars, television and refrigerators. Peaceful coexistence did not therefore mean an end to the rivalry between capitalism and socialism. It meant only that this rivalry should not escalate into war. In Khrushchev's words:

37 Nikita Khrushchev with Mao Zedong in Beijing, 1958. The smiles conceal serious disagreements between the two communist leaders. Mao led the opposition to Khrushchev's policy of peaceful co-existence.

We are in favour of a détente but if anybody thinks that for this reason we shall forget Marx, Engels and Lenin, he is mistaken. This will happen when shrimps learn to whistle. We are for coexistence because there is in this world a capitalist and a Socialist system but we shall always adhere to the building of Socialism. We don't believe that war is necessary to that end. Peaceful competition will be enough. (Michael Balfour, *The Adversaries*)

So much for the theory. The reality proved to be rather different. The United States and the Soviet Union did not go to war but they came very close to it while Khrushchev was in office. Why?

The reasons are varied and often complicated but perhaps the main one is that Khrushchev found himself under enormous pressure. His attack on Stalin and his idea of peaceful coexistence landed him in trouble with Communist China. Mao Zedong signed a Friendship Treaty with Stalin in 1950 but the two sides were hardly firm allies. Mao resented the lack of Russian support during the civil war in China, and also the way in which Stalin left China to fend for itself against the Americans during the Korean War. China had a long-standing border dispute with the Soviet Union and claimed several thousand square miles of Soviet territory as its own. Mao also strongly disagreed with Khrushchev's attack on Stalin and the idea of peaceful coexistence.

Khrushchev's attack on Stalin was followed almost immediately by demonstrations in Poland and a revolution in Hungary, which was only put down when Soviet tanks appeared on the streets of Budapest. Mao argued that the attack on Stalin was undermining the very basis of communist rule in Eastern Europe. On coexistence, Mao clung to Lenin's idea that war was inevitable between capitalist and socialist countries. Khrushchev's argument that war was unthinkable in the nuclear age made no impression on him. With larger populations, Mao believed that the Soviet Union and China and the other socialist countries would be able to survive a nuclear war. Khrushchev was horrified by such views. As he recalled in his memoirs:

I was too appalled and embarrassed by his line of thinking even to argue with him. To me, his words sounded like baby talk. How was it possible for a man like this to think such things? For that matter, how was it possible for him to have risen to such an important post? (Talbot, ed., *Khrushchev Remembers*)

Khrushchev's differences with Mao led to many disputes between the Soviet Union and China. The Russians withdrew their advisers from China and cancelled plans to help China develop an atomic bomb. The Chinese for their part accused the Russians of 'revisionism'. They argued that the Russians were betraying the ideals of the communist movement. The Russians in turn accused the Chinese of 'dogmatism', of clinging to out-of-date ideas. As the quarrel simmered in print and at party conferences, the Soviet Union found that its leadership of the communist world was being challenged.

In the meantime, Khrushchev faced more serious problems closer to home. The Berlin problem was a constant thorn in his side. He wanted a settlement under which the Western powers would finally agree to recognize the government of East Germany. He said that the 1945 agreements about the status of Berlin were obsolete. On several occasions he threatened to sign a separate peace treaty with

East Germany. Under such a treaty, the Soviet Union would transfer its control over all communications between West Germany and West Berlin to the government of East Germany. The Western powers would then have to negotiate their access rights to West Berlin with East Germany. In effect, they would have to recognize East Germany.

Khrushchev visited the United States in 1959 and had talks with President Eisenhower. It was then agreed that a conference should be held at Paris in 1960. The conference failed before it started. It collapsed as a result of the U-2 incident, when the Russians shot down an American U-2 spy plane which was taking photographs of missile sites in the Soviet Union. Khrushchev then had talks with President Kennedy at the Vienna summit in 1961. Their talks ranged over a variety of issues and Kennedy raised the danger of a nuclear war arising from a miscalculation. Khrushchev flew into a rage and shouted at the president:

Miscalculation! Miscalculation! Miscalculation! All I ever hear from your people and your correspondents and your friends in Europe and every place else is that damned word, miscalculation. You ought to take that word and bury it in cold storage and never use it again. I'm sick of it! (William Manchester, *Remembering Kennedy: One Brief Shining Moment*)

38 Soviet tanks parade through Red Square on the anniversary of the Russian Revolution, November 1957. Russia's conventional forces were formidable but her nuclear forces were inferior to those of the United States. Khrushchev boasted about Russia's military strength and attempted to conceal her nuclear inferiority from the West.

In August 1961 Khrushchev adopted his own solution to the Berlin problem. He dropped the idea of a separate peace treaty with East Germany. Instead he approved the construction of the Berlin Wall. He had to act. The exodus of people from East Germany was rebounding on the Soviet economy. The Soviet Union depended on East Germany for high technology products and equipment such as machine tools, chemical products and electrical appliances. In return, the Russians provided East Germany with raw materials and energy supplies of oil and natural gas. East German exports to the Soviet Union had fallen dramatically in the years leading up to the Berlin Wall in 1961. Khrushchev therefore acted to protect the Soviet economy as well as East Germany. As the Wall went up, the world held its breath. American and Soviet tanks squared up to each other at Checkpoint Charlie, one of the crossing points which divided the Eastern and Western sectors in Berlin.

Defence was Khrushchev's other great problem. In 1957, the Soviet Union scored a couple of notable firsts. It became the first country to put a satellite – Sputnik – into space, and it also became the first country to test successfully an intercontinental ballistic missile (ICBM). The Russians scored another notable first in 1961 when Yuri Gagarin made the first manned space flight. The reaction in America to Sputnik and the ICBM was almost one of panic. Assuming the Russians to be ahead in the field of technology, many Americans believed that a 'missile-gap' had opened up. They feared that they were open to an attack because the Russians had greater strike-power. But the missile-gap did not exist. The Americans were still vastly superior because of their long-range bomber force. They also began to produce their own ICBMs.

Khrushchev exploited the missile-gap idea and he often boasted about Russia's military strength. But he knew that the Americans were superior. He also knew that Kennedy had begun his presidency by spending vast sums on defence. By 1962, the year of the Cuban missile crisis, the Americans had already developed a three-to-one superiority

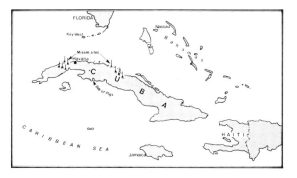

39 Map of Cuba showing the location of the Bay of Pigs and the Soviet missile sites.

in intercontinental and submarine-launched ballistic missiles. This more realistic version of the missile gap placed Khrushchev in a dilemma. To close it, the Soviet Union would have to spend huge amounts on defence. The domestic economy, particularly Khrushchev's plans to produce more consumer goods, would inevitably suffer. In an attempt to escape his dilemma, Khrushchev took his greatest gamble. He decided to put Soviet missiles on Cuba. Khrushchev acted in part to protect Cuba against another American-backed invasion. But he also had another motive. He wrote in his memoirs:

In addition to protecting Cuba, our missiles would have equalized what the West likes to call the 'balance of power'. The Americans had surrounded our country with military bases and threatened us with nuclear weapons, and now they would learn just what it feels like to have enemy missiles pointing at you; we'd be doing nothing more than giving them a little of their own medicine. And it was high time America learned what it feels like to have her own land and her own people threatened. (Talbott, ed., *Khrushchev Remembers*)

The key point here was the idea of equalizing the balance of power. With their own missiles on Cuba, just 90 miles off the coast of Florida, the Russians would be able to neutralize America's ICBM superiority. If they succeeded, the Russians would be spared the need to spend vast sums building a new generation of ICBMs. Khrushchev's domestic reforms might therefore be saved. But the

plan did not succeed. Confronted by firm American opposition, Khrushchev had no alternative but to back down.

Khrushchev put a brave face on the Cuban missile crisis. He even claimed it as a victory. He wrote in his memoirs:

The resolution of the Caribbean crisis came as a historic landmark. For the first time in history, the Americans pledged publicly not to invade one of their neighbours and not to interfere in its internal affairs. This was a bitter pill for the US to swallow. It was worse than that: the American imperialist beast was forced to swallow a hedgehog, quills and all. And that hedgehog is still in its stomach, undigested. No surgical operation to remove the hedgehog is possible as long as the Soviet-American agreement on Cuba is in effect. (Strobe Talbott, ed., *Khrushchev Remembers*)

Others saw it rather differently. The Chinese had a field-day. They accused the Russians of reckless behaviour in putting the missiles on Cuba in the first place and then cowardice in removing them. The Chinese were also angered by the 1963 Test Ban Treaty. They refused to sign it.

Time was now running out for Khrushchev. The quarrel with China had split the communist world. Communist countries and communist parties began to take sides. The Soviet Union was no longer the undisputed leader of world communism. The German problem remained unsolved. At home, Khrushchev's economic reforms had failed to produce the results expected of them. Many conservative members of the Soviet Communist Party believed that Khrushchev's attack on Stalin, although cautious and limited, had gone too far.

On holiday by the Black Sea in October 1964, Khrushchev was summoned back to Moscow by the Presidium. He was told that he had been dismissed. He lived out the rest of his life in obscurity just outside Moscow. To the new Soviet leadership of Leonid Brezhnev and Alexei Kosygin, Khrushchev had become a 'non-person'. With a superb sense of timing, just two days after Khrushchev's dismissal, the Chinese successfully tested their first atomic bomb.

Fidel Castro (1927-   )

Fidel Castro is one of the longest serving rulers in the world. He came to power in Cuba in 1959 when his revolutionary '26 July Movement' overthrew Fulgencio Batista, Cuba's right-wing dictator. Since then Castro has emerged as Cuba's left-wing dictator, ruling his country with an iron hand and proving himself a thorn in the side of both superpowers. Castro and Cuba played crucial roles when the Cold War reached its height at the end of the fifties and the early sixties.

The son of a sugar planter, Castro studied law at the University of Havana in the Cuban capital. As a lawyer in the late forties he defended the poor of Havana in a number of court cases. He also became a left-wing political activist and led an armed revolt against the Batista regime on 26 July 1953. Hence the name of his revolutionary movement. The revolt failed and Castro spent two years in prison. Freed as part of a general amnesty he went into exile in Mexico where he began preparing a guerrilla campaign against Batista. He returned in secret to Cuba in December 1956 with his brother Raul and Che Guevara, the legendary Latin American guerrilla fighter who was killed in Bolivia in 1967. Castro's revolutionary movement soon began to attract popular support. Batista contributed to his own downfall. His regime was so oppressive that it lost the support of the Cuban army and the United States, Cuba's main arms supplier. Batista had to flee the country at the end of 1958, leaving Castro to make a triumphant entry into Havana on 8 January 1959.

Castro did not come to power as a communist. It was not until 1961 that he declared himself a Marxist-Leninist. But from the beginning Castro was determined to wipe out the economic and social injustice of what he described as Cuba's 'underdevelopment'. Tad Szulc, author of a biography of Castro, describes what the Cubans mean by underdevelopment:

To Fidel and the revolutionary generation, underdevelopment means illiteracy and disease, economic inadequacy, dependence on the West under the shackles of 'neo-colonialism', and above all, the thinking patterns of people in poor countries. To him and his disciples, underdevelopment is shame, it is third- or fourth-class citizenship in the world. (Tad Szulc, *Fidel: A Critical Portrait*)

Castro began a crash programme of educational reform – to build more schools, train more teachers and bring down the rate of illiteracy. At the time of the revolution, barely 40 per cent of the six million Cubans could read and write. But Castro's ambitious social reforms needed money and his plans for economic reform led to conflict with the United States.

The Cuban economy was dominated by foreign interests. American companies controlled about 80 per cent of Cuba's public services and 40 per cent of the sugar crop, Cuba's principal export. Castro nationalized the foreign companies and introduced land reforms designed to give land to the Cuban peasants. He also began to look elsewhere, to the Soviet Union and Eastern Europe, for foreign aid. The Russians were quick to capitalize on the situation. They agreed to buy half of the Cuban sugar crop (2.7 million tons) at a price above the world market. The East Europeans bought another 1.3 million tons. Russian and East European advisers began arriving in Cuba to build new industrial plants.

These developments alarmed the Americans. Cuba is only 90 miles off the coast of Florida. The Americans feared that the Cuban revolution might be exported abroad – to the neighbouring states of Central and Latin America. During the final months of the Eisenhower administration, the CIA began planning an invasion of Cuba to overthrow Castro. The idea was not to commit American troops. Instead, the Americans provided the training

40 Fidel Castro makes a triumphant entry into Havana, the Cuban capital, following the overthrow of Batista in 1959.

41 Castro with Khrushchev. As in the case of Mao Zedong, the smile and hug conceal serious differences. Castro resented the terms which Khrushchev accepted to end the missile crisis in 1962.

and the weapons for about 1500 Cuban exiles, who were based at camps in the Central American republic of Guatemala. The exiles came from rich or middle-class families. Some had served as soldiers and officials under Batista. The CIAs plans had reached an advanced stage when John F. Kennedy began his presidency in January 1961. Kennedy had serious doubts about the operation but he allowed it to go ahead.

Castro knew that an invasion was about to happen. He had already built up a highly efficient intelligence apparatus. Cuba was put on a war footing, and Castro took personal charge of the military plans to repel the invaders. The invasion force came ashore in the early hours of Monday 17 April 1961 on the beaches of the Bay of Pigs, but it was spotted almost immediately and the news conveyed to Castro. The Cuban leader proved himself a master strategist. Castro had correctly anticipated the invasion plan and he ordered his small air force to attack the support fleet which had landed the invaders.

Kennedy more or less condemned the invasion to failure by his refusal to provide air cover for the fleet. The Cuban air force was able to inflict decisive damage on the ships,

with the result that the invaders who came ashore were cut off from supplies. The invaders put up a brave fight but they were soon forced to surrender. The entire operation had lasted about 24 hours. In Cuba, Castro's popularity soared and he became a national hero.

Castro extracted maximum political advantage from his victory. He presented it as a victory for the Cuban revolution over the forces of imperialism. He made a four-hour appearance on Cuban television, during which he told the story of the invasion using maps and captured documents. But he was also generous in his hour of triumph. Only fourteen of the captured exiles were brought before a revolutionary court and charged with pre-revolution crimes. Of these only five were executed. The vast majority of the prisoners were released and allowed to leave Cuba at the end of 1962, in return for supplies of food and medicines from the United States.

The Bay of Pigs affair shaped future relations between Cuba and both super-powers. The Americans continued to regard Castro as a dangerous revolutionary. The CIA plotted to assassinate the Cuban leader. Kennedy refused to approve a political killing but after the President's own assassination in 1963 the CIA made several unsuccessful attempts on Castro's life. Castro himself viewed Kennedy's death as a tragedy. He did not blame Kennedy for the Bay of Pigs. He also considered that it was fortunate for Cuba that Kennedy was president at the time. Years later Castro wondered what might have happened if Richard Nixon had succeeded Eisenhower. Nixon had been Eisenhower's vice-president and he was Kennedy's Republican opponent during the 1960 presidential election. In an interview with Tad Szulc in 1984 Castro remarked:

And even though he launched the invasion, I think that Kennedy had great merit. If it had been Nixon, I am convinced that he would not have resigned himself to the defeat of the invasion, and there would have been an escalation, and that in this country we would have been trapped in a very serious war between North American troops and the Cuban people . . . the man who had the personal qualities, who had the personal courage to realize that a great error had been committed, to calm himself and to hold himself back – this man was Kennedy. So, if we had an invasion that was prepared by Nixon and Eisenhower, we also had the luck that a Nixon was not elected to the presidency, and that at that moment it was a Kennedy, who was ethical, who was president. (Szulc, *Fidel*).

Relations between Cuba and the Soviet Union after the Bay of Pigs were more complicated. Although the victory had been achieved by Cuban soldiers and airmen, Castro was quick to acknowledge that the Cuban armed forces had been supplied with weapons by the Soviet Union and its East European allies. Cuba was now part of the socialist camp. Also, although Kennedy ruled out a political killing, Cuba still lived under the threat of another American-backed invasion. It was for this reason that Castro welcomed the decision to install Russian missiles in Cuba. Khrushchev of course had his own motives, but for Castro the missiles were needed to ward off another invasion.

Imagine therefore Castro's reaction when, at the height of the missile crisis in 1962, Khrushchev agreed to remove the missiles from Cuba. Castro was angry, for two reasons. First, because Khrushchev had not told him that the Americans had more missiles. As Castro recalled later:

At that time I did not know how many nuclear weapons the Soviets had and how many nuclear weapons the North Americans had. I did not know it, and it did not occur to me to ask the Soviets about it. It did not seem to me I had the right to ask: 'Listen, how many missiles do you have, and how many do the North Americans have, what is the balance of strength?' We simply trusted that they, for their part, were acting with knowledge of the entire situation. We did not have the information to be able to make a complete evaluation, we only received a part of the information. (Szulc, *Fidel*)

The second reason for Castro's anger was that Khrushchev did not keep him informed about the negotiations with the Americans which led to the removal of the missiles. He was particularly irritated to discover that the Russians had done a deal with the Americans, removing the missiles from Cuba in return for an American promise to remove some rather old American nuclear missiles from Turkey. Castro felt that his country had been treated as a pawn in the game of superpower competition and he was not satisfied with Kennedy's pledge to respect Cuba's independence.

The Cuban missile crisis strained relations between Castro and the Russians. Both sides still needed each other. Cuba was in desperate need of economic aid which only the Soviet Union and the Eastern bloc were willing to supply. But equally, the Russians needed the Cubans. They could never afford to break their relations with Cuba because they feared that they would be replaced by China. It would be wrong therefore to describe Cuba as a Soviet satellite. Castro still had considerable room for manoeuvre in his dealings with the Russians. Both sides continued to utter public declarations of friendship but behind the

42 Flanked by Laebua Jonathan (left), the prime minister of Lesotho, and Samora Michel, the president of Mozambique, Castro hosts the sixth non-aligned summit meeting at Havana, September 1979.

scenes they frequently disagreed. The terms of Russia's economic aid to Cuba and the question of how to respond to Third World revolutions (Castro was always more inclined to support them than the Russians) were frequent sources of dispute.

Relations between Cuba and the Soviet Union remained strained until 1969. They then began to improve, in part because Castro supported the Russians over their invasion of Czechoslovakia in 1968. Also, in the 1970s, the Russians became more adventurous in supporting Third World revolutions. Cuban troops, together with Russian and Eastern bloc military and technical advisers, intervened to tilt the scales in favour of communist factions in Africa, notably in Angola. They also helped the Marxist government of Ethiopia in a war against neighbouring Somalia. But Castro was still determined to play an independent role in the Third World. His crowning moment came in 1979, when Havana played host to a meeting of the Non-Aligned Movement of Third World countries and Castro was elected chairman of the movement, a position he held until 1982.

Today, Castro and Cuba face many problems. At home, the revolution has lost much of its early idealism. The Cuban economy is still dependent on outside aid and there are rumblings of political discontent over Castro's centralized system of government. Castro shows no signs of copying Mikhail Gorbachev's domestic reforms, but abroad the Cuban leader has been forced to pay heed to Gorbachev's desire to end regional disputes. As part of an agreement with South Africa to enable Namibia in South-West Africa to become independent, the Cubans have withdrawn their troops from Angola.

John Fitzgerald Kennedy (1917-63)

John Fitzgerald Kennedy seemed to have everything. He was young and handsome. He had a glamorous wife and two young children. He had wealth and the backing of one of the most prestigious families in America. He had served as a torpedo-boat commander in the Pacific during the Second World War and he had been decorated for bravery. In January 1961 he became the youngest and first Roman Catholic president of the United States. His presidency lasted 1037 days. On 22 November 1963 he was shot dead by a sniper's bullet as he rode in a motorcade through the streets of Dallas, Texas.

Kennedy began his presidency with a call to action. He declared in his inaugural address:

Let every nation know, whether it wishes us well or ill, that we shall pay any price, bear any burden, meet any hardship, support any friend, oppose any foes, in order to assure the survival and success of liberty. This much we pledge – and more. (Stephen Ambrose, *Rise to Globalism; American Foreign Policy since 1938*)

Kennedy was seen as a symbol of hope and inspiration. His stirring speeches contained memorable phrases. 'Freedom', he declared at the beginning of his presidency, was under 'the most severe attack it has ever known.' The great battleground for the defence and expansion of freedom was the Third World, in Kennedy's words, 'the whole of the southern half of the globe – the lands of the rising people.' Kennedy declared that he was 'not satisfied as an American with the progress we are making.' He wanted the people of Latin America, Africa and Asia 'to start to look to America, to what the President of the United States is doing, not . . . Khrushchev or the Chinese Communists.'

Kennedy had emphasized these themes during his election campaign. He attacked Eisenhower and the Republicans. They had promised much but delivered little. For all the brave talk of liberation and massive retaliation, Eisenhower had been cautious – too cautious for Kennedy's liking. By the end of the fifties, communism and the national liberation struggle in the Third World appeared to be on the march. Sputnik and the ICBM seemed to suggest Soviet superiority in the field of technology. Kennedy urged immediate action to correct this impression. He also wanted the United States to regain the initiative abroad which the Republicans seemed to have lost.

To demonstrate American superiority, Kennedy launched America's space programme. The Russians had put the first man in space but Kennedy was determined that the Americans would be the first to put a man on the moon. He also approved an enormous increase in defence spending. His military budget soared to 56 billion dollars. Kennedy inherited from Eisenhower 200 ICBMs. By 1964, a year after Kennedy's death, the number had risen to 834 (by the same date the Russians had only 200).

The president also increased the strength of America's conventional forces. He was convinced that the major threat to peace lay in communist support for insurgency wars or, as the communists called them, wars of national liberation. Special emphasis was placed on the training of elite counter-insurgency units, like the Green Berets who fought in South Vietnam. It was under Kennedy that the United States took the crucial steps towards full-scale military intervention in Vietnam. When Eisenhower left office in 1961, there were 500 American military advisers in Vietnam. By the end of 1963 there were about 16,000 'advisers'.

Kennedy had more pressing problems during his first year in office. He bitterly regretted having authorized the Bay of Pigs invasion. Three weeks after the fiasco he received a letter from Khrushchev inviting him to a summit at Vienna. Kennedy thought of postponing the summit but changed his mind because he realized that this would be seen as a sign of weakness. The Vienna meeting was the most difficult encounter of Kennedy's life but he stood his ground when Khrushchev flew into a rage over the question of a miscalculation setting off a nuclear war. Khrushchev was wearing a number of medals. Kennedy reached over, touched one and asked what it was for. Taken aback, Khrushchev proudly declared that it was the Lenin Peace Prize. Kennedy replied calmly: 'I hope they let you keep it.'

43 John F. Kennedy with Khrushchev at the Vienna summit, June 1961. The Soviet leader is wearing the Lenin Peace Medal which Kennedy referred to during one of Khrushchev's outbursts.

Kennedy refused to give in to Khrushchev's threats over Berlin but he agonized over the whole question of the German problem. Just before the Berlin Wall was built Kennedy said privately:

All wars start from stupidity. God knows I'm not an isolationist, but it seems particularly stupid to risk killing a million Americans over an argument about access rights on an autobahn in the Soviet zone of Germany, or because the Germans want Germany reunified. If I'm going to threaten Russia with a nuclear war, it will have to be for much bigger and more important reasons than that. Before I back Khrushchev against a wall and put him to a final test, the freedom of all of Western Europe will have to be at stake. (William Manchester, *Remembering Kennedy*)

44 Berlin flashpoint. A privately owned car, with American military number plates, crosses back into the American sector of Berlin at Checkpoint Charlie, October 1961. On its return journey the car was stopped by East German guards. It was only allowed to proceed across the border when two American jeeps drove up behind it. American tanks stand guard on either side and in the foreground.

In 1963, two years after the Wall went up, Kennedy visited West Berlin. Standing on a platform before a huge crowd he delivered what was perhaps the most memorable speech of his life:

There are many people in the world who really don't understand, or say they don't, what is the great issue between the free world and the communist world.
Let them come to Berlin!
There are some who say communism is the wave of the future.
Let them come to Berlin!
And there are some who say in Europe and else-where that we can work with the communists.
Let them come to Berlin!
And there are even a few who say that it is true that communism is an evil system, but it permits us to make economic progress.
Let them come to Berlin!
All free men, wherever they may live, are citizens of Berlin, and therefore, as a free man, I take pride in the words: 'Ich bin ein Berliner!' [I am a Berliner]. (Manchester, *Remembering Kennedy*)

The crowd became hysterical. Kennedy, at first exhilarated by the occasion, became alarmed. He felt sure he would have been obeyed had he urged the crowd to tear the Wall down.

But the Cuban missile crisis represented Kennedy's sternest test as President. The crisis began in Washington on 14 October 1962 when a U-2 flight produced unmistakeable photographic evidence that missile sites were being constructed on Cuba.

The news was not made public. Kennedy appointed a special committee to advise him. It was known as the Executive Committee or Ex Comm for short. Robert Kennedy, the Attorney-General and the president's younger brother, was one of the key members.

The Ex Comm saw six possibilities. The first was to do nothing, but this was not a serious option. American opinion was so agitated about the threat of communism that inaction on Kennedy's part might well have led to his impeachment. The second possibility – diplomatic action through the United Nations – was dismissed because it would be too time-consuming. It might also have been counter-productive. As more Third World countries became members of the United Nations, the United States could no longer rely on automatic support in the UN General Assembly. Putting pressure on Castro was a third possibility but this was dismissed because Castro was not directly responsible for the missiles.

Three courses of action were left – a blockade of the ships carrying the missiles to Cuba, an air-strike to destroy the missile sites, and an invasion of Cuba. The last two had strong supporters in the Pentagon, America's Defence Department. But Robert Kennedy urged a less aggressive response. His arguments won the day and the Ex Comm decided in favour of a blockade.

The missile crisis now became public. Kennedy explained the background in a

45 One of the aerial surveillance photographs which the Americans used to prove that the Russians were building missile sites on Cuba, 1962.

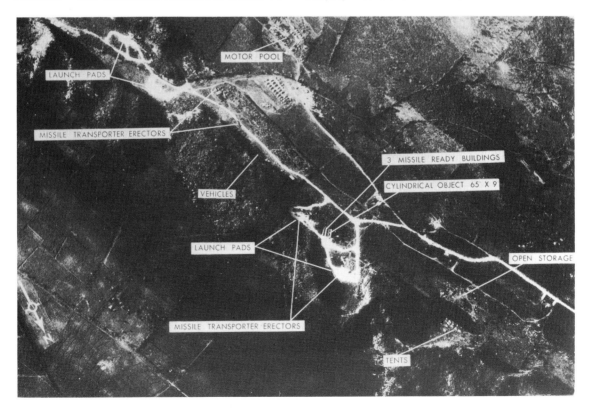

televised address on 22 October 1962. He also announced what action he was taking:

To halt this offensive build-up, a strict quarantine on all offensive military equipment under shipment to Cuba is being initiated. All ships of any kind bound for Cuba from whatever nation or port will, if found to contain cargoes of offensive weapons, be turned back. This quarantine will be extended, if needed, to other types of cargo and carriers. We are not at this time, however, denying the necessities of life as the Soviets attempted to do in their Berlin blockade of 1948. (David Rees, *The Age of Containment*)

For the next six days, as Soviet ships steamed towards Cuba and the American navy was deployed to intercept them, the world waited and held its breath. Khrushchev's first reaction to Kennedy's measures was one of outrage. He accused the United States of 'banditry'. Several letters were exchanged between the White House and the Kremlin. On 26 October Khrushchev sent a letter to Kennedy. It was long, rambling and emotional. It was clearly written by a man under tremendous pressure. 'If war should break out', the letter read, 'then it would not be in our power to stop it.' Khrushchev said that he would send no more weapons to Cuba and that he would withdraw or destroy those already there if Kennedy agreed to end the blockade and promised not to invade Cuba. On 27 October the Ex Comm met to consider its response. But on the same day, and before the Ex Comm had reached a decision, a second letter arrived from Khrushchev. It was more formal than the first and it raised the price for a settlement of the crisis. Presumably under pressure from the Soviet military, Khrushchev now said that he would remove the missiles from Cuba if Kennedy ordered the removal of American missiles stationed in Turkey. 'You are worried over Cuba', Khrushchev stated:

You say that it worries you because it lies at a distance of 90 miles across the sea from the shore of the United States. However, Turkey lies next to us . . . . You have stationed devastating rocket weapons . . . . in Turkey literally right next to us. (Ambrose, *Rise to Globalism*)

The Ex Comm was stunned. This was an impossible demand. The missiles in Turkey were old and Kennedy had already decided to remove them. But Kennedy could not remove them under Soviet pressure. This would be a blow to American prestige. The Joint Chiefs of Staff in the United States urged an air strike against Cuba. The Ex Comm seemed ready to accept the inevitable but Kennedy wanted to wait at least one more day.

Robert Kennedy then came forward with a suggestion that the Ex Comm should ignore Khrushchev's second letter and send a reply accepting the solution which he had suggested in his first. Kennedy accepted his brother's suggestion and a letter was sent to Moscow. At the same time Robert Kennedy had a meeting with Anatoly Dobrynin, the Soviet Ambassador to the United States. Dobrynin raised the question of the American missiles in Turkey. Robert Kennedy explained the American position. The United States would not accept any arrangement made under threat or pressure. But he also said that once the Cuban crisis had been resolved, the missiles in Turkey would be removed. This was sufficient for the Russians. On 28 October Dobrynin informed Kennedy that the missiles in Cuba would be withdrawn. Amidst considerably less publicity, the American missiles in Turkey were removed in 1963.

President Kennedy's prestige and popularity soared to new heights because of his handling of the missile crisis. But he was unable to capitalize; he was gunned down just over a year later. His death shocked the entire world. But it seems unlikely that he would have been able to change the subsequent course of history had he lived. Kennedy had nudged the United States a significant step closer to the Vietnam war and the Russians were determined to build a nuclear arsenal to match that of the Americans. Individuals such as John F. Kennedy can leave their mark on history but they are still products of the forces at work and the spirit of the times in which they live.

DATE LIST

1943

April	Discovery of mass grave at Katyn Forest in Poland.
May	Comintern dissolved.
November-December	Tehran Conference

1944

July	Soviet Union sets up Lublin Committee in Poland
July-October	Warsaw Uprising
October	Churchill and Eden visit Moscow
December	Civil War begins in Greece

1945

February	Yalta Conference
April	Roosevelt dies; Truman becomes president
May	Germany surrenders
June	United Nations Charter signed
July	United States detonates atomic bomb
July-August	Potsdam Conference British general election; Clement Attlee, Labour leader, replaces Winston Churchill as prime minister
August	Atomic bomb dropped on Hiroshima (6 August) Soviet Union declares war on Japan (8 August) Atomic bomb dropped on Nagasaki (9 August) Japan surrenders (15 August)

1946

February	Kennan's Long Telegram
March	Churchill's Iron Curtain speech
April	Elections in Czechoslovakia Socialist Unity Party (SED) set up in Soviet zone of Germany
June	Referendum in Poland
July-October	21-nation Peace Conference opens in Paris
September	James Byrnes, American Secretary of State, announces at Stuttgart that Germans should become responsible for their own affairs and that American troops will remain in Germany

1947

January	United States and Britain establish bizonia in Germany Communist-controlled elections in Poland
February	Peace Treaties signed with Italy, Romania, Bulgaria, Finland and Hungary
March	Truman Doctrine
June	George Marshall announces Marshall Plan in Harvard speech
June-July	Meeting in Paris of British, French and Soviet foreign ministers to consider Marshall Plan; Molotov walks out (2 July)
July	Conference of 16 European countries in Paris to plan Marshall Aid; Committee on European Economic Cooperation set up Kennan's 'Mr X' article about containment published in *Foreign Affairs*
August	Defeat for Smallholders (Peasant Party) in Hungarian elections
September	Nicola Petkov, leader of Bulgarian Peasant Party, executed Cominform established
October	Peasant Party dissolved in Romania Mikolajczyk flees Poland
December	King Michael of Romania abdicates

1948

February	Communist takeover in Czechoslovakia
February-March	London conference of America, Britain, France and Benelux countries on future of West Germany
March	Death of Jan Masaryk Russians withdraw from Control Council in Germany
June	Western powers announce currency reform for West Germany Berlin blockade begins Yugoslavia expelled from Cominform

1949

January	Soviet Union establishes Comecon (Council for Mutual Economic Assistance) to co-ordinate economic policies in Eastern Europe
April	North Atlantic Treaty signed in Washington
May	Berlin blockade ends
July	Soviet Union detonates an atomic bomb
September	Federal Republic (West Germany) established
October	Victory for communists in China's Civil War German Democratic Republic (East Germany) established

1950

January	Klaus Fuchs arrested in Britain
February	Senator Joseph McCarthy alleges he has the names of 205 communist sympathizers employed in the State Department
May	Robert Schuman, French foreign

	minister, proposes European Coal and Steel Community (ECSC)
June	Outbreak of Korean War
October	René Pleven, French prime minister, proposes a European Defence Community (EDC)
1951	
July	America, Britain and France formally end state of war with Germany
1952	
March	Soviet Union proposes a united but neutral Germany
May	EDC Treaty signed in Paris
July	ECSC established
November	United States detonates H-bomb
	Eisenhower elected president
1953	
March	Death of Stalin
June	Uprising in East Berlin
July	Korean Armistice signed
August	Soviet Union detonates H-bomb
1954	
April-May	Trial of Oppenheimer
May	French defeat in Indo-China
August	French Assembly refuses to ratify EDC Treaty
1955	
May	West Germany joins NATO
	Warsaw Pact established
	Austrian State Treaty establishes Austria as a neutral state
	Khrushchev and Bulganin visit Yugoslavia
July	Geneva summit
1956	
February	Twentieth Congress of Soviet Communist Party at Moscow

June	Demonstrations in Poland
October-	Hungarian Revolution
November	Suez crisis
1957	
March	Rome Treaty establishes European Economic Community
August	Russians test ICBM
October	Sputnik launched
November	Conference of Communist Parties at Moscow: debates over revisionism and dogmatism
1958	
November	Khrushchev's first Berlin ultimatum
1959	
January	Castro in power in Cuba
June	Khrushchev renounces atomic agreement with China
September	Camp David meeting in US between Eisenhower and Khrushchev
1960	
May	U-2 incident; Paris summit collapses
November	Kennedy elected president
1961	
April	Bay of Pigs landings in Cuba
	Yuri Gagarin's first manned space flight
June	Vienna summit between Khrushchev and Kennedy
August	Berlin Wall built
1962	
October	Cuban missile crisis
1963	
June	Hot Line agreement
August	Test Ban Treaty signed
November	Kennedy assassinated
1964	
October	Khrushchev dismissed
	China tests atomic bomb

BOOKS FOR FURTHER READING

Elizabeth Campling, *The USA since 1945*, Batsford, 1988.

Elizabeth Campling, *The USSR since 1945*, Batsford, 1990

Brian Catchpole, *A Map of Our Own Times*, Heinemann, 1983

Michael Dockrill, *The Cold War 1945-1963*, Macmillan, 1988

Peter Fisher, *The Great Power Conflict after 1945*, Blackwell History Project, 1987

Charles Freeman, *The Superpowers*, Batsford, 1990

Peter Lane, *Europe since 1945*, Batsford, 1985

Harriet Ward, *World Powers in the Twentieth Century*, Heinemann, 2nd edition, 1985

INDEX